A CHRONICLE OF CLIFTON AND HOTWELLS

a chronicle of
CLIFTON
and
HOTWELLS

HELEN REID

REDCLIFFE
Bristol

First published in 1992 by
Redcliffe Press Ltd
49 Park St, Bristol.

© *Liz Marleyn*

ISBN 1 872971 36 9

British Cataloguing-in-Publication Data.
A catalogue record for this book is available
from the British Library.

Typeset and printed by
The Longdunn Press Ltd, Bristol.

Contents

Introduction

This book does not set out to be a scholarly study of Clifton and Hotwells. It is a social history, charting the ordinary everyday life of this fascinating suburb.

Alongside the factual narrative, I have assembled a patchwork of trivia, from newspapers, advertisements, diaries, novels, poems, letters and reminiscences, with the hope of providing verbal snapshots that give the flavour of everyday life in Clifton and Hotwells from the eighteenth century to the present day.

How did the residents live, what did they wear, what were their houses like, what did they do for entertainment? Where did they shop, what kind of education did they have, how did they treat their servants – and what made them so angry that they wrote to the editor of the *Clifton Chronicle* about it?

In fact the things they complained about are astonishingly familiar: the state of the roads and the pavements, cruelty to animals and vivisection, noise and litter, begging, the felling of trees, the loss of vital shops, Sunday trading, the rudeness of the younger generation, empty properties going to rack and ruin, and the state of the poor. Human nature does not change all that much.

The area has not changed a great deal physically either. Any ghost from the eighteenth century would find parts of Clifton and Hotwells perfectly familiar, and a nineteenth century one would find the suburb largely unaltered.

This continuity is what local historians find so absorbing, hence the mass of research done by others before me. The sources are too numerous to list – they run into hundreds – but thanks must go to Bristol United Press for many of the illustrations.

In addition to the Bristol United Press, the author wishes to thank the following sources of illustrations, by picture number.

Bromheads 54; City of Bristol Museums and Art Gallery 3, 4, 8, 9, 20, 21, 24, 25, 26, 28, 31, 35; Clifton College 46; Gordon Kelsey 22; Museum of The Batheaston Society 80; John Trelawny-Ross 40, 44, 45, 78; The University of Bristol 58.

"A Strange Hot Well"

It takes an heroic effort of imagination to visualise modern traffic-battered Hotwells as the height of elegance and fashion.

But Hotwells between 1760 and 1790 was THE place to go if you wanted to mingle with the titled and famous, attend a ball, take breakfast at one of the Long Rooms with the Earl of Jersey, and then go to take the waters.

If you took an imaginary carriage ride – it will cost only 6d – from College Green to the Hotwell in the summer of 1775, you would leave along Frog Lane and so into Limekiln Lane, which followed the line of the modern St. George's Road.

This was the centre of Bristol's booming building industry and where famous architects such as the Paty family, plasterer Thomas Stocking, as well as the decorators, masons, glaziers, and carpenters, lived and had their yards. Timber, bricks, stone and marble was landed on the wharves by Anchor Lane; The Limekiln Glasshouse, by Gas Ferry Lane, and Child's Glasshouse on Mardyke, provided window glass, and bottles for the Hotwell and the lime kilns dotted at the foot of Brandon Hill and on the slopes of Clifton Wood, by now part of the Goldney estate, produced the lime for mortar, whitewash and plaster.

You jolted along this rough unmade road which was bad enough to produce a 'Disgusted of Hotwells' letter after an accident in 1792, sarcastically informing the Merchant Venturers: "So long as the mud remains, coaches will fall in a soft surface and consequently nothing but smothering remains to be dreaded." There were already continuous houses (since demolished by road widening) on the Clifton Wood side of the Hotwell Road, and from the Mardyke on the other, all the way to Hotwells, by 1775 quite recognisable as today's suburb.

From Sketchley's trade directory of 1775, it is possible to reconstruct the occupations of the people who lived and worked there. Hotwells folk depended on the docks, the building trade and tourism for a living. There were five carpenters, three sawyers, a glassmaker and a wheelwright, a hallier (delivery man) and a smith and two gardeners serving the building trade, a staymaker, three shipwrights and four captains working for the Port. William Champion had built his graving dock where Merchants Road is now, in 1765, providing more work for locals, and his floating harbour scheme was taken over by the Merchant Venturers in 1770, and enlarged in 1776. Hotwells people did not rely on tourism alone.

The travellers and workers needed refreshment and there were already 11 alehouses and inns in Hotwells at this stage. (The record was to be 32). Three of them are still trading, the Plume of Feathers, the Bear, which was a coaching inn, and the Adam and Eve.

Catering for the locals and the tourists to the Well were three tailors, three peruke makers, a milliner, a dressmaker, a laundress, a soapmaker, five shoemakers, and for provisions there was a gingerbread baker and three ordinary bakers, a brewer, three butchers, four grocers and tea dealers.

Five post chaise men ferried the visitors about, and seven medical men looked after them. They were the apothecaries, who were the equivalent of today's pharmacists, and who charged for medicines but not for advice, the barber surgeons, who treated fractures and injuries and bled patients at the request of physicians, who alone had to be university graduates. They lived in the best houses in Dowry Square and Chapel Row.

Most of the traders of Hotwells doubled as lodging keepers as there was always a big demand: Sketchley lists 20 lodging and boarding house keepers in the area, and there were also two hotels, the York in Dowry Square and the famous Royal Gloucester Hotel, on the site of the Haberfield Almshouses and demolished in 1874. It was remarkable because it consisted of two houses, one built on the top of the other. The hotel had a 90 ft. Long Room where breakfasts and suppers were provided, and there was a rival New Long Room opposite which also catered for visitors.

Lebeck House, where Carrick House flats now stand, was first a lodging house run by Mrs Mead, who in 1740 published her trade card: "Mrs Mead respectfully informs the nobility and gentry that she has suits of apartments at the above house, elegantly furnished at the most moderate terms."

The house was so named after a famous London chef, and was run from 1754 by Elizabeth Trinder of Lebeck's Head Tavern in Bath: she announced she

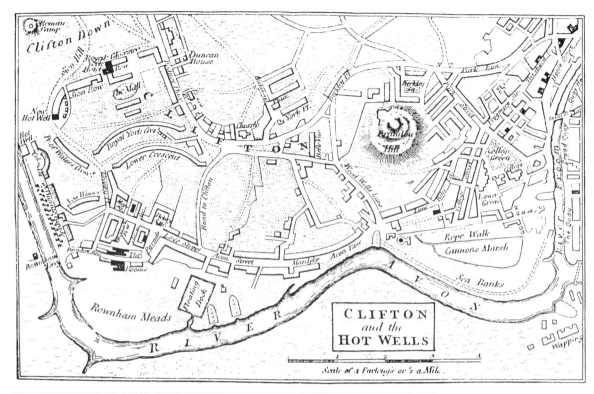

1. & 2. Clifton and Hotwells around the turn of the eighteenth century, and how the great artist, J.M.W. Turner saw the Hot Well.

8

had "opened a house at the Hotwells for the reception of company as a tavern or eating house." She offered "an ordinary (a set lunch) every day at three o'clock at half a crown a head (12p) the house being the first of its kind attempted here."

Traders from Bath, and indeed from London, would set up shop during the Hotwell season, which was May to October: Mrs Ann Walton, the Bath milliner and M. Pierre Joly, late Head Cook to the Duke of Devonshire gave their services and in 1743 Robert Goadsby had a bookshop at Bath and another at Hotwells and opened them alternately, according to the season – Bath's followed on Bristol's, and most visitors moved on, liking the contrast between the comparatively rustic outdoor Hotwell, and the indoor formality of Bath.

London lace dealers came down with their wares to tempt the throng walking in the Dowry Square pleasure grounds, which then extended all the way along to the end of Dowry Parade, selling lappet heads for ladies from six guineas and ruffles for gentlemen from two guineas. By the Hotwell itself and on the route up to Clifton, naturalists would set up stalls selling minerals and "spars" and Bristol diamonds made into jewellery. On the corner of Granby hill was Mrs Miller's sweet shop.

Running a lodging house soon became the economic mainstay of the area near the Hotwell and it is plain even today, with rooms in connecting pairs, that most of the eighteenth century housing was built precisely for this purpose. On each of the main floors, the front room was the parlour, with connecting doors to a bedroom at the back. Visitors would rent one or two floors, or the whole house if they were rich, and be waited on by the landlady and her servants, who cooked and did the laundry in the basement and slept in the attics. Dowry Square, Dowry Parade, Albemarle Row, Hope Square, and St. Vincent's Parade were all designed with this in mind.

The Dove House in Dowry Square (no 9) was advertised in 1748 as being "built on purpose for lodgings, having below stairs two large kitchens and servants' hall, both sorts of water (spring and rain, drinking and non-drinking) and all other conveniences." A house in this fashionable square could be rented for £80 a year; weekly rates for an apartment were from 10s, or 16s with board. Servants, put in attic rooms, cost half price.

Unimaginably, Hotwells in the eighteenth century was chic: this was a district fit for landed gentry and

for famous literary and artistic figures, and it attracted what was called in the contemporary press a fashionable throng.

Clifton, except for the area round the top of Clifton Hill, where the rich merchants built their mansions, came into being mainly because of tourism at the Hotwell, for Hotwells was already a well-established suburb when Clifton was still a tiny village with a church, farms and smallholdings, and a scattering of fine houses.

Hotwells is the much older suburb, Iron age and Roman settlements apart; it was the first place where the Avon could be forded and Rownham ferry dates back to at least 1148, when the crossing was the property of St. Augustine's monastery – the Abbot used it as the most direct way to his house at Abbot's Leigh.

Although there are no buildings left earlier than 1700, Hotwells was certainly inhabited by the sixteenth century, and benefiting from the dock and shipbuilding trade, because the wills of seamen and building workers mention that they own "tennyments" on the Hotwell Road, on the slopes of the Clifton wood. These trades provided work long before Hotwells took to spa life, but it was the Hotwell itself which put the place on the map.

The Hotwell spring was first mentioned by the fifteenth century topographer William Wyrecestre, and was said by sailors to be a cure for leprosy. Bristol diamonds, which were not diamonds at all but quartz of magnesian conglomerate, were sufficiently famous to get mentioned in poems and plays of the seventeenth century. Two thousand of them were supplied by Sir John Young of Bristol to King James I to decorate his palace, Theobald's.

By the early seventeenth century the Gorge, St. Vincent's Rock, the Bristol diamonds and the spring were famous enough to attract visitors from afar, witness the Three Cavaliers of Norwich, who wrote a famous account of it in 1643, John Evelyn who came in 1655 and compared the scenery to the Alps, and the unhappy queen Catherine of Braganza, a visitor in 1677.

The water's fame had spread too: Dr. Samuel Ward, a Cambridge don from 1610–1634, was advised to drink the water and had it shipped via the Severn, and in 1626, Sir Hugh Smythe of Ashton Court was "rising early to go to the well."

Defoe noted in 1724 that the water, in glass bottles made down in Limekiln Lane, was sent all over the world, and in the 1730s, it was regularly

3. Quarrying in the Gorge beneath St. Vincent's Rock (wash drawing by I.W. Upham, 1802).

4. St. Vincent's Rocks and the Hot Well in 1785, by Nicholas Pocock, Bristol's best known marine artist.

sent by sea to London and advertised in the London press. It was also sold on the streets in Bristol, for unlike Bath water, the Hotwell water did not deteriorate in bottle.

By then doctors were beginning to write about the therapeutic value of the Hotwell spring, and clearly the place was ripe for exploitation.

The first attempt to commercialise the spring came in 1630 when John Bruckshaw obtained a 40 year lease from the Crown to mine the rocks for gold, silver and crystal gold and to take the Hotwell water and make baths for the use of those who frequent the spring.

His petition read: "John Bruckshaw has found a fountain or spring of water issuing from a high rock adjacent to the sea in the Western part of the kingdom, which cures many diseases far beyond any known bath in the kingdom. It lies between high water and low water mark."

The water was given a great boost in 1680 when Abel Gagg, a Bristol baker, claimed it had cured his diabetes, after a dream that he had drunk plentifully of the spring, and recovered (Bristolians were greatly given to dreaming important information).

At first there was just a brick enclosure round the spring, which came out just beyond the Clifton pier of the Suspension Bridge; at high tide the spring would be flooded and polluted by river water, which of course contained raw sewage.

When the lease ran out, the Merchant Venturers, who had acquired the land, granted in 1695 a 90 year lease to Charles Jones, a soap boiler and Thomas Callow Hill, a draper, for an annual fee of £5, provided that they spent £500 on developing the area, with a pump room, lodgings and walks, and a proper pumping system with valves, to prevent contamination, and in 1696 the first pump room, known as the Hotwell House was built out over the river and the spring.

Another boost to the water's popularity came when doctors began to endorse it for the treatment of tuberculosis, then a major and incurable disease. But most people came for social reasons, to see and be seen, rather than for their health. They came to gossip and dance and promenade, and to ride on the Downs. "Every fine Sunday the place is like a fair, vast numbers coming from Bristol and all around to drink the water", wrote an observer in 1754.

The point to aim for on the Downs was the Ostrich Inn, famous for its breakfasts for visitors to the Hotwell, many of whom rode there, two to a horse, to play on the bowling green; dinners with turtle soup could be had at short notice and on Sunday there was an ordinary, a set lunch for 1s. a head for excursionists from Bristol. The house was so popular that landlord William Evans erected lamps on the Downs.

It was only when the invalids began to outnumber the pleasure-seekers that the spa began to decline. Paradoxically it was a reputation for curing consumption that was partly responsible for the failure of the spa.

But in its heyday, 1760–1790, the Hotwell evidently became famous abroad because some eighteenth century prints have captions in French as well as English. *Felix Farley's Journal* lists well over 700 names of visitors in 1776. "The season at the Hotwell is now truly brilliant."

The New Vauxhall Gardens, which must have stood under the Cumberland basin flyover, attracted 2,000 people on its opening day in 1743. There were concerts, fireworks, plays, and shopping expeditions and one of the great charms of the place were the low prices and the brilliant company. Bristolians loved to come and gawp.

So why didn't Clifton develop in parallel? In 1750 there were only about 20 houses in Clifton and even in 1780, at the height of the Hotwell's fame, there were scarcely more than 30 upper class houses, scattered along from the top of Clifton Hill to the Green.

The mundane answer is that Clifton was impossibly difficult to get to, on foot, on horseback, or in a carriage. There were four ways to it: via the toll road, which came over the Downs, past where the Zoo was later to be built to the tollhouse, and then along the line of the modern Promenade; from the Gorge there was a pre-Roman winding footpath roughly where Bridge Valley Road is, and there were the 200 steep and slippery steps, which started behind the Colonnade and went straight up along the border of what is now the garden of the Avon Gorge Hotel – the Zig Zag was not built until 1829.

Other routes up were Granby Hill, named after the Marquis of Granby who visited in 1744, a steep road hacked out of the rock and as late as 1816 described as "a precipitous track" which terrified people, and Woodwell Lane, modern Jacobs Wells Road, also a rutted rocky climb, which led to the steep Clifton Hill. Until McAdam brought his road-making skill to Bristol, these roads were genuinely frightening, especially to invalids.

5. The poets waxed eloquent.

This was probably why Boyce's Buildings, speculatively built by Bath wigmaker Thomas Boyce in 1763 to provide lodgings for the spa, failed to attract custom and made him bankrupt. The journey up and down was too much for people who were ill.

Boyce spent £8,000 on his grand terrace of three houses, with its pleasure garden, three summer houses, ten coach houses and stabling for 34 horses. *Felix Farley's Journal* said it was "a building of very superior description and with offices evidently designed for the accommodation of a first rate character, and which has confidently been stated was intended for residence by George III." The project was completed in June 1772 and he went bust the following November. The present mutilated building had a third of it chopped off when

Merchants Road was built in 1858.

The difficulty of getting to Clifton also explains why comparatively few of the aristocratic Hotwell visitors met the merchants living in the mansions on the hill. The main tourist traffic seems to be have been to Goldney House, to see the famous garden and grotto, started in 1723 and worked on for 20 years. A ticket was obtained from the gardener, Adam Sixsmith, who showed visitors round the walks with their painted scenery, the follies and the artificial cave.

Landscape was an eighteenth century obsession and early visitors to the Hotwell all write about the Gorge in what seems to us extravagant and romantic terms – John Evelyn said it was confragious as the Alps, and Pope enthused about the scenery,

6. The Gorge was a perennially popular subject for the artist. This study by Robert Wilkins is uncannily similar to the better known Pocock drawing.

7. This nineteenth century watercolour by Samuel Jackson shows the Gorge partly tamed by quarrying.

though Doctor Johnson, ever crusty, wrote of "Bristol's barren rocks."

What we see now is no guide: both sides of the Gorge are virtually man-made. Ceaseless quarrying (there were five quarries on each side), the removal of outcrops for safety reasons, work on railway cuttings and tunnels, or on building roads, has altered its character, making it less craggy, narrow and winding.

Until 1816, St. Vincent's Rock protruded almost to the brink of the Avon, and at high water there was only a narrow path on the verge of the river, to allow towage of vessels, but in 1816–17, to alleviate the distress of the poor, labourers were hired to quarry the projecting rock away. In this century the banks have been raised and the entire Gorge widened, for the building of the Portway from 1922.

And the sheep have gone. The slopes of Nightingale Valley were still grassy in 1831, because it was grazed. The romantic aspect of the scenery – the hanging woods and flowery dells – has diminished because the entire ecology of the Gorge has changed since sheep grazing was abandoned, early this century. Views which Turner, Danby and Samuel Jackson painted are now obscured by trees. From Leigh Woods they could still see the Clifton rooftops.

The sheep finally vanished altogether in 1924, after an outbreak of disease, but as late as 1872 there were 300 to 400 of them grazing on the green, and in 1909 the manager of the Clifton Down Hotel in Sion Place was complaining that the continual bleating annoyed his guests.

In addition, Victorian development of high density housing meant that seeds and seedlings migrated from gardens into the Gorge and colonised the slopes, taking over the grass, furze, gorse and wildwood. The Downs too have changed from being up to the late eighteenth century quite rough common land with furze and bracken into something more like a park, and the interesting and rare flora and fauna have all but disappeared: the landscape has been tamed.

Yet in the seventeenth and eighteenth centuries the Avon Gorge was considered to be one of the great natural wonders of Britain.

But as well as admiring the scenery, the visitors wanted more sophisticated entertainment, and one of the diversions of the Hotwell was the theatre; Gay's *Beggar's Opera* had 50 performances in the Long Room in 1728, and the following year the

THE AVON GORGE DELINEATED

By the Haven's channel we found a strange Hotwell which came gushing and pouring out of a mighty stony rock into the stream so nigh thereto by a rocky and steep winding and craggy way near 200 slippery steps, which place when the tide is gone now wants good store of company to wash in this and to drink that warm medicinable water, and for its rarity diverse carry some away with them.
When we had felt and tasted the rare excellency of these waters, we mounted up again and for the space of an hour or two turned pioneers, to dig and delve for some glittering bastard stones which that hill plentifully afforded.

Account by the Three Cavaliers of Norwich, 1634.

THE FAMOUS FLYER

Thomas Kidman the famous flyer who has flown from several of the highest precipices in England, flew on Monday last from the highest of the rocks near the Hotwell at Bristol, with fireworks and pistols, after which he went upon the rope and performed several surprising dexterities on it in the sight of thousands of spectators.

The Weekly Miscellany, April 17th, 1736.

POPE'S EYE VIEW

Passing still along by the river, you come to a rocky way on one side, overlooking green hills on the other; on that rocky way rise several white houses and over them red rocks mixed with green bushes and of different coloured stone. This at a mile's end terminates in the house of the Wells . . .
When you have seen the hills which seem to shut in upon you, you go into the house (the pump room) and look out at the back door. A vast rock of 100 foot high, of red, white green, blue and yellowish marble all blotched and variegated, strikes you quite in the face, and turning on the left there opens the river at vast depth below, winding in and out and accompanied on both sides with a continued range of rocks up into the clouds of a hundred colours, one behind another.

Alexander Pope, letter of 1739.

QUARRYING

Here men are daily employed in blowing up the rock with gunpowder; vast fragments are frequently thrown down and repeatedly strike the precipice with dreadful crash, and with loud report of the explosion re-echoed from side to side by the lofty cliffs, make a grand and awful noise which resembles thunder and it sometimes by strangers mistaken for it ... but if the blowing up of these rocks still continues the design (Vick's bridge across) will be rendered impracticable; and also their venerable appearance and grandeur will be diminished.

***Matthews Directory* 1793–4.**

TAKING A BATH

When a person goes into the little room where the bath is, he takes the key of the door with him and taking hold of the iron rings which are fastened in the walls, he steps backward down two or three steps, dips his head under the water two or three times and afterwards stays in, perhaps five or ten minutes. Every person that goes in pays a shilling a time and the bath is filled afresh for every person, every time he bathes.

***A Description of Somersetshire*, 1769.**

ON THE WATER'S CURATIVE POWERS

For on notice that this water has done some good against the stone, people of all sorts repair unto it, so well as have not the stone as those that have it or stand in fear thereof, and abundantly glut and fill themselves therewith till they vomit and start again. Therefore I would have you know that the ill and preposterous use thereof will weaken the stomack, subvert the liver, annoy the head and breast, occasion Cramps, pain the joynts, breed crudities, rheums, coughs, cachexies, the Dropsie itselfe, and Consumption.

***Thomas Venner's Censure*, 1637.**

SOME ASTONISHING CURES

Consumption: William Darvise of West Street, Lawford's Gate, Bristol, aged 53, at the last extremity consumptive, a frightful skeleton, continually coughing, straining and spitting day and night, appetite gone, sleep with his physicians vanished and his friends hourly expecting his death, by drinking the Hotwell water this present summer is to astonishment restored to appetite and sleep, hale and active, without cough or any remaining symptoms.

Diabetes: Mrs Flemming, South Parade, Bath, aged 70, corpulent and tall, laboured under great thirst, parched tongue, fever and flux of urine, so that her strength was greatly impaired and her flesh much wasted. I persuaded her to go to Bristol where by drinking the water for one fortnight her tongue became moist, her urine lost its sweet taste and was reduced to its natural quantity.

Stone and Gout: Mr Martin, purser of a ship was afflicted with a diarrhoea for six years. He was also subject to gravelish complaints voiding great quantities of fabulous matter. By drinking the water two months only he was completely cured of both ailments.

External Disorders: Miss Lancaster of Castle Green at six years old had the King's Evil running at one finger, out of which came a bone, with a running in her left cheek and left hand, her foot and toes hard and cruelly swelled. By drinking, bathing and medicines intermixed, she was cured.

Famous cures reported by Dr. Alex Sutherland, 1763.

TAKING THE CURE

I believe the Bristol waters at the Well would be serviceable if I could stay long enough, viz six weeks or two months, for as they are an Alternative and of no great strength, they require a longer time to operate than warmer and more impregnated mineral waters such as Bath etc. The place is so Exposed and so inconvenient for want of Chairs, Coaches at all easy etc., that there is no living long here in winter for such thin bodies as mine.

Alexander Pope, 1739.

Peachum in that production, Wookey character actor John Hippisley, decided to build the first provincial purpose-built theatre at Jacob's Wells (roughly where the upper block of modern flats is). It was safe from proscription being just outside the city boundary, and conveniently next door to an alehouse.

An advertisement in the *London Weekly Journal*, 1728 announced: "We are now building a spacious theatre at Limekilns, lying convenient for coaches as well as the Rope Walk (the footpath from the Cathedral along the river bank) leading to the Hotwell." It opened on June 28th with Congreve's *Love For Love*. Hippisley himself wrote a hit comedy, *A Journey To Bristol*, and put it on there in 1731.

It was about a wife who wanted her liberty to go to the Hotwell, and see a play. "O horrid", says her husband, "the devil and all his works. The Long Room is a school of Wickedness and the Playhouse a Nursery to the Devil. 'Tis at those places that women learn to load their husbands' heads (with cuckold's horns) and lighten their pockets."

The Playhouse was completely finished by 1736, in an oblong shape with a gallery above and seats on stage: it was later enlarged to an amphitheatre shape, with boxes all round. Chatterton called it a hut but the theatre, enlarged in 1747, was big enough for Shakespeare performances, so long as actors exited from one side and ran round the back outside to get on the other side.

Going to the Playhouse was quite an adventure: there were often fights, drink was handed to members of the audience – and the cast – through a hole in the wall, and the pickpockets waited on Brandon Hill when the performance was over, so that the theatre had to provide linkmen to light patrons' way back to College Green.

Hippisley died in 1748 and his widow, and then his actress daughter Jane Green, carried on running the theatre; it closed in 1757, reopened in 1758, staggered on with pantomime, variety and circus, after the rival the Theatre Royal opened, and closed for good in 1771. The building was demolished in 1803.

What the Hotwell was always seeking was the social style of Bath, but it never really achieved it. And while the water at Bath to this day is considered to have curative properties, the Hotwell water was largely discredited by the end of the eighteenth century.

As to whether the water ever really did have any healing powers, it is not possible for modern scientists to tell, since the original spring cannot be found, and in any case the water may have since changed its character. In 1912 the spring was discovered to be highly radioactive, which may explain why invalids felt it did them so much good!

Though it evidently did not cure consumption or diabetes, it is quite possible that it helped with digestive and urinary disorders and skin complaints. Drinking the slightly diuretic water in large quantities would have flushed out the kidneys at least, and this in turn would help with digestion; in an age when washing was optional, daily baths in fresh warm water would be bound to help cure skin complaints.

Add to this the healthy outdoor exercise – riding horseback on the downs, strawberry picking in Ashton fields, picnics on the river, walks, and so on, and it is obvious that a sense of well-being and relaxation made people feel better. And compared with most eighteenth century medical treatments, the water cure was mercifully painless. There must have been a placebo effect as well.

It seemed to have worked for John Wesley who in 1754 visited not the fashionable Hotwell House but another rival spring at the New Hotwell, much further up the Gorge. "When he first came his countenance looked as if a greedy consumption had determined to put an end to his days. But in less than three weeks he was enabled to set out on the Cornish circuit". Wesley himself attributed his recover partly to the treatment and partly to "plaster of brimstone, white of egg and that old unfashionable ingredient, prayer." There were other rival springs, from 1786 at the Tennis Court House (later Poole's coal wharf) on the Mardyke, and at Sion House from 1793, though neither attracted much custom.

Up to this time, the charges at the Hotwell were reasonable but in 1784 the Merchant Venturers advertised for new tenants and required them to spend heavily on repairs and improvement. Samuel Powell who took over in 1790 did the work, but put up the charges considerably, with the result that the number of visitors suddenly declined. Even so, 32,000 bottles of Hotwell water were sold nationwide in 1795, at 6s. a dozen, and £1,330 taken in subscriptions to the Pump Room.

But this was not the only reason for an almost overnight slump. The start in February 1793 of the Napoleonic war, and the recession it caused, the

GLOUCESTER HOUSE & STEAM PACKET HOTEL

LATE BARTON'S

Clifton Hotwells

George Warne, begs to announce to the Nobility, Gentry and Public in general, that he has taken the above spacious and commodious Hotel, and respectfully solicits a continuance of the favors which have been for many Years past, conferred on his predecessor; trusting by strict attention to the comfort of those Ladies and Gentlemen who may honour him with their support; & by making moderate charges to merit the same.

EXCELLENT WINES & SPIRITS, BOTTLED BEER, PORTER, CIDER & PERRY, WHOLESALE & RETAIL.

A good & well supplied Larder with Turtle in the season.

The above Hotel from its contiguity to Cumberland Bason where the Steam Packets lie, affords every convenience to Persons passing to or fro by them, and FAMILIES *will find this House particularly calculated for their accommodation.*

Dinners, Suppers, made-dishes, and Soups, sent out at the shortest notice.

EXCELLENT STABLING WITH GOOD LOCK UP COACH HOUSES, POST-HORSES, CHAISES, LANDAUS &c.

Coaches to all parts of the Kingdom.

8. A superb trade card for the celebrated Gloucester Hotel, where the affluent visitors
to the Hot Well stayed.

THE USUAL METHOD

The usual method of taking the water is to go to the pump room in the morning and take a glass of it which contains half a pint and then to sit down with the company about half an hour. A band of musicians perform every morning during the season; each person who chooses subscribes five shillings to them.

For those who prefer exercise to sitting there is a colonnade with shops built under the rocks and a gravelled parade about 800 feet long, shaded by trees, by the side of the River so that the company may enjoy a dry and pleasant walk when it rains or an airy cool and shady walk in the warmest season: also during the influx and efflux of the River, they may be entertained with the sight of the ships and vessels that pass up and down.

There are two very large elegant public rooms, the one called the Old or Upper Long Room, kept by J. Barton; the other which is opposite, is called the Lower or new Long Room, kept by Foreman. At these rooms are public breakfasts, during the season, every Monday and Thursday alternately, with cotillions and country dances, for which each person pays 1s.6d. The balls are on Tuesdays. Subscriptions for walking in the rooms and gardens, and reading the newspapers, is 5s. and for the balls one guinea; this is at each room.

E. Shiercliff: *The Bristol and Hotwell Guide, or Useful Entertaining Companion*, **1789.**

HOW DID IT TASTE?

Those who would have it in perfection should drink it at the spring, where it has a delicate soft milky taste beyond that of any medicinal water that is known in England. It appears perfectly pellucid, and though it is so warm and soft to the taste, it is in reality hard and will not dissolve soap equably, but curdles it into white masses. It will not wash linen or extract the virtue of tea so well as common water, but after exposure to the air for about three weeks or longer, it will answer these purposes full as well.

It leaves a sensation of dryness on the palate, is perfectly without smell, pleasing and grateful to the stomach, cooling and quenches thirst.

Matthews Guide 1793–94.

THE FIRST NEW VAUXHALL

In the evening we went to a pretty garden near the Hotwells which they call Vauxhall. There are some booths and pleasant arbors hung with some globe lamps etc, an orchestra wherein were a good band of musicians. There was no company there this night, which rendered it very disagreeable and several times after but few. The Poor Man who owned it was at great expense to keep it in order, and but a short time after was obliged to decamp.

Description by an Irish Gentleman, 1752.

THE SECOND NEW VAUXHALL

They have here furnished up an old family seat [Clift House?] and built a salon in length 75 feet. The gardens were luckily laid out before so some lamps stuck about there needed no more. Six days out of seven business begun is ended in jolly feasting and fun. Nights are given up to fine suppers on which tradesmen squander all their profits. I saw a breeches maker defending his fair cheeks from the sun with a pink silk umbrella and another shopkeeper renowned for his drinking, mirth and song, swaggering with a large oaken stick, a slouch'd hat and black stock, cropt hair, leather breeches and jockey cut frock.

Hotwell's New Vauxhall Gardens, a satirical description, **May 1776.**

EFFECTS OF THE LISBON EARTHQUAKE, 1755

The water in the well became red as blood and so extremely turbid that it could not be drunk, all conjectures concerning the cause were in vain. I once met with a person who pictured the consternation it created, being considered an omen of the world's final slaughter. All flew to the churches where incessant prayers were offered to avert the apparent approach of their destruction and to appease the rage of heaven.

Fugitive Sketches of Clifton **by S.W. Manby, 1802.**

9. The Hot Well promenade, where 'the company may enjoy a dry and pleasant walk when it rains . . .' (aquatint after J.C. Nattes, 1804).

medical advances which made people more sceptical, the terrible reputation the hordes of consumptives gave the spa, and the challenging medical theories of Dr. Thomas Beddoes, all contributed to the decline. After the war was over and prosperity returned, England had a fashionable Prince Regent and attention turned from spas to the health-giving sea bathing. Those who believed in spas could once more travel abroad to the grand Continental ones.

Although the old Hotwell House was demolished in 1822 and a new Pump Room in Tuscan style was built in an attempt to revive the spa, it never was the success it had been in the eighteenth century and the buildings were finally demolished in 1867, so that the Hotwell promontory could be blasted away to give the big ships safer passage through the Gorge.

All that remains now is a sordid little cave in the rock, just beyond the Colonnade, where the handsome pump stayed until World War I. It was then removed to the City Museum, who at the outbreak of World War II sent it to the Underfall Yard, whence it disappeared, possibly to become part of a Spitfire.

The Hotwell's fine days were over, and the suburb went into a steady decline which has persisted almost to this day. In the great days of the spa, Clifton was described as being "at the Hotwell." But by 1830, the Hotwell was "at Clifton."

And while Hotwells sank, Clifton began to rise.

10. Humphry Davy.

11. Dr Thomas Beddoes.

12. Samuel Taylor Coleridge.

13. Robert Southey.

"Sent there to die"

The Hotwell in its prime attracted the literary set – Pope, Addison, Cowper, Gay, Sheridan and Mrs Thrale all visited. By the end of the eighteenth century, the scientists began to arrive too.

One of them, Dr. Thomas Beddoes, indirectly and unintentionally contributed to the medical downfall of the Hotwell. Beddoes dismissed the idea of treating tuberculosis with a water cure and turned to air as a remedy for the disease that was to challenge medical researchers until into the middle of the twentieth century.

Dr. Thomas Beddoes arrived in Hotwells in 1793, to set up an experimental laboratory in the basement of 11, Hope Square. Erasmus Darwin had suggested Hotwells because of the plentiful supply of consumptive patients, and at Hope Square, where he stayed until 1799, Beddoes was investigating new gases, with an apparatus designed by James Watt.

His experiments worried the neighbours who petitioned his landlord to get rid of this peculiar tenant, who did unspeakable experiments on kittens, treating them with pure oxygen, then drowning them to see how quickly they could be revived.

In 1799 Beddoes moved to 6, Dowry Square to join Humphry Davy at the Pneumatic Institute, "intended for the treatment of diseases hitherto found incurable. The application of persons in confirmed consumption is principally wished at present," said their opening advertisement in the *Bristol Gazette*. The establishment was supported entirely by subscriptions from liberal men of science, and curious intellectuals came long distances to find out what was going on there.

Their assistant was Peter Roget, later of Thesaurus fame; his job was to record the types of persons susceptible to consumption. There was no shortage of patients desperate for a cure and at the beginning the Institute was a great success, having eight in-patients and 80 out-patients.

The treatment used gases, delivered in an airbag, and also digitalis and miniate of lime, and after the 1799 discovery of the Voltaic Pile, continuous electric current, or galvanism. They built a treatment box rather like a sedan chair, in which the patient would sit, breathing in nitrous oxide, or laughing gas.

Davy used to experiment on himself and had several narrow escapes, at times rushing out up the steps for fresh air and throwing himself on the grass behind Dowry Square. He describes how he would dose himself to the limit and then wander down by the Avon, where he fainted. "I was quickly restored and I endeavoured to make a bystander acquainted with the pleasure I experienced by laughing and stamping."

All their literary and scientific friends, Coleridge, Southey, Thomas Wedgwood, Tobin, Joseph Priestley, Maria Edgeworth, tried the gas: they were of course, quite innocently, getting 'high'. Maria Edgeworth called it "gas which inebriates in a most delightful manner, having the obvious effects of Lethe and at the same time giving the rapturous sensations of the nectar of the Gods." Southey said it made him laugh and tingle in every toe and fingertip. "Davy has invented a pleasure for which the language has no name."

Their behaviour must have shocked the locals. "The only motion I felt inclined to make was that of laughing at those who looked at me," said Coleridge. Maria described "a woman who when she tried it, dashed out of the house, leaped over a great dog in the way, but being pursued by the fleetest of her friends, the fair fugitive, or rather temporary maniac, was at length overtaken and secured without further danger." Davy discovered the gas was an anaesthetic for toothache – and indeed it is still used in dentistry.

Life in Dowry Square between 1798 and 1801 when the Institute closed, must have been highly interesting. Wild rumours about what went on at no. 6 spread about: one said that 10,000 dogs that Davy and Beddoes had ordered for experiments had escaped onto the Bristol quay.

Though Beddoes believed that oxygen machines would soon become ordinary articles of household furniture, no one was cured of consumption; nothing worked, not the water or the gas or the galvanism, or breathing in cow's breath, as the graves in the Strangers' Burial Ground, opened in 1787, testify. Desperate consumptives from all over the country and even from abroad, who had come to the Hotwell as a last resort, were buried there, and ironically, Beddoes himself also was laid to rest

14. & 15. The Pneumatic Institute at Number 6 Dowry Square, where Humphry Davy and friends had a jolly time sniffing nitrous oxide.

16. The 'curious subterranean recess': Mr Goldney's famous grotto was a popular venue for visitors to the Hot Well.

along with the tubercular strangers, in 1808.

And, strangely, four years later another inventor interested in using gases arrived in Dowry Square. In 1812, Jacob Schweppe from Switzerland came to Bristol to set up a shop to sell his discovery, soda water – and to produce, as he advertised "artificial mineral water and Bristol Hotwell water impregnated with air" to make it fizzy.

But by then the Hotwell had been discredited, and the start of the Napoleonic war had added to the slump at the spa. But not before a building mania had hit Clifton, the area where tourism from the Hotwell had expanded, because of the shortage of lodgings down below. The charms of airy Clifton as a holiday resort were ripe for development.

The population figures tell the story: in the seventeenth century Clifton was mainly agricultural, and inhabitants numbered about 80 in 1608. The few houses there were – the farm and the manor house, but not the church – were burned down in

1645 by Prince Rupert's troops during the civil war, so that even in 1712, the population was only 450.

In 1766, the population was 1,500, in 1770 1,365, in 1784, 2,205. But thanks to "the rage for building" which was first reported in 1786, the population of Clifton had doubled to 4,457 by 1801.

In those years, started but not necessarily finished were Park Street, Great George Street, Berkeley Square and Crescent, Sion Row, the Mall, Rodney Place, Princes Buildings, Windsor Terrace, Royal York Crescent, Saville Place, Cornwallis Crescent, and Bellevue. (Many of these terraces demonstrated the current belief that people should live as far away from ground level as possible to avoid rheumatism, hence the raised walks over deep basements and cellars).

The terraces were unfinished because the merchants who had invested their money in speculative building found that the Napoleonic war hit their trade with Europe and caused a slump in business at

23

17: A scene from Fanny Burney's *Emelina*, a novel partly set in Clifton
and the Hot Well.

Bristol docks; from 1793 to 1815 there was a local recession, and the building boom caused people like architect Francis Greenway and shot-manufacturer William Watts to go bankrupt.

Royal York Crescent was started by the creation of a tontine in 1790 but in 1793, 34 of the houses were roofless shells, with mantraps set inside to catch lead thieves. The War Office wanted the houses as barracks for the militia, for 2,000 of them were lodged at inns, paying only a halfpenny a day, but there were strong protests from residents and by 1818 most of the houses were completed.

Cornwallis Crescent was still unfinished by 1824; Saville and York Places had gaps and Richmond Terrace had several unoccupied houses when in 1799 a gang of thieves attempted to steal lead from the roof. "They were only prevented when one of the gang being caught in a mantrap, which from the quantity of blood left on the trap and the premises, must have severely wounded him."

Bellevue had eight unfinished houses offered for sale in 1810: the problem was that the speculators sold on unfinished houses to other speculators or to small builders who were unable to complete the work, or went bankrupt doing so. Some of the houses fell down and had to be rebuilt. In all, at the worst point of the slump, some 500 houses in Clifton were empty or unfinished. Tyndall's Park had been sold in 1790 for the building of an extensive Bath-style crescent but the war caused the project to collapse.

One of the saddest casualties was Francis Greenway, who went bankrupt speculating in unfinished houses. He was deported to Australia in 1813 for fraud and forgery: he had contracted with a Colonel Dobson to finish 34 Cornwallis Crescent for 1,300 guineas but he later claimed it had been agreed to pay him an extra £250. But the documentary proof Greenway produced was forged. In the end, it was Australia's gain, for he went on to design some of New South Wales's best classical buildings. But before his downfall, he did design the Mall's splendid if now over-altered Clifton Assembly Rooms, with the attached Clifton Hotel.

In 1805 a wealthy French Huguenot J.W. Auriol (his coat of arms is on the pediment) purchased the site and Greenway designed the rank of buildings. The Assembly Room opened in 1806 and the hotel in 1811, with "a ball and a feast for the citizens, who were presented with an ox roasted whole." It had 70 bedrooms, 20 sitting rooms, and attracted an exclusive clientele.

Very probably Jane Austen visited the Assembly Rooms with her mother, when they stayed in Clifton in July 1806. Maddeningly there is no record of where they lived, though one theory is that it was with friends in Gloucester Row. She later wrote to her sister Cassandra: "It is two years tomorrow since we left Bath for Clifton, with what happy feelings of escape."

The hotel added Royal to its title in 1830 when the Duchess of Kent and her young daughter, Princess Victoria aged 11 came to stay; the royal party occupied a suite on the first floor and attended a ball in the Rooms; she is also supposed to have walked down the newly established Zig Zag – a lot to fit into one day.

By the end of the Napoleonic Wars, Clifton was gradually being settled as a permanent suburb: what more sure sign but the formation in 1818 of a gentlemen's social club, whose home since 1857 has been the Assembly Rooms itself.

As a health resort famous for its air, Clifton became a retirement spot for ex-army and navy officers, clergy, professional men, the artistic set and the minor gentry, who judging from the early nineteenth century tombstones in the parish churchyard, came from all over the world, from the colonies, Ireland, America even, to settle in Clifton in their old age. Only the farmworkers and servants and the merchants on Clifton Hill were actually locals, and this social mix, augmented by visitors, made Clifton a lively and interesting village in the Regency period.

Even with building mania, it was still very rural, with hayfields in Caledonia Place, a farm at Litfield, and a dairy in Richmond Place. There was a pound for strayed animals and a dewpond on Bobby's Field, and there were no houses at all between Clifton Down and the toll house at the junction of Bridge Valley Road, near where the Zoo now has its entrance.

Pembroke Road was still Gallows Acre Lane (the last execution at the gibbet at the top was in 1783) and at the junction with Queen's Road was a wild flower haven known as Flower Hill. Whiteladies Road was a lane with extensive market gardens and nurseries either side, one long stretch being owned by Garaway, a firm still going strong in the same area.

Not everyone approved of Clifton's expansion. "The Bristol people have done all in their power to

A JAUNDIC'D VIEW

I rode out upon the Downs last Tuesday, in the forenoon, when the sky, as far as the visible horizon, was without a cloud; but before I had gone a full mile, I was overtaken instantaneously by a storm of rain that wet me to the skin in three minutes – whence it came the devil knows; but it has laid me up (I suppose) for one fortnight. It makes me sick to hear people talk of the fine air of Clifton downs: how can the air be either agreeable or salutary, when the demon of vapours descends in perpetual drizzle?

I was t'other day much diverted with a conversation that passed in the Pump-room, betwixt my uncle and the famous Dr. L---n, who is come to ply at the Well for patients. My uncle was complaining of the stink, occasioned by the vast quantity of mud and slime which the river leaves at low ebb under the windows of the pump-room. He observed that the exhalations arising from such a nuisance could not but be prejudicial; to the weak lungs of many consumptive patients who come to drink the water. I have read all that has been written on the Hot Wells and what I can collect from the whole is that the water contains nothing but a little salt, and calcarious earth, mixed in such inconsiderable proportion as can have very little, if any effect on the animal economy. This being the case, I think, the man deserves to be fitted with a cap and bells for such a paltry advantage as this spring affords, sacrifices his precious time which might be employed in taking more effectual remedies, and exposes

himself to the dirt, the stench, the chilling blasts, and perpetual rains that render this place to me intolerable.

Smollett's *Humphry Clinker*, published 1771. [Smollett visited Hotwells in 1766]

---

ruin the rural beauty of Clifton Hill by the number of abominable Buildings they have erected all over it," complained Lady Hesketh in 1799.

The big houses now had large parcels of land: Goldney's included most of the Clifton Wood, Henry Hobhouse at Cornwallis House had all the land now occupied by Royal York Villas, and Royal York Crescent was built on the site of a large orchard owned by the Rev. Power.

Clifton Court, home of the porcelain works owner Richard Champion, and now the Chesterfield, had the land now the Fosseway, and a long-vanished mansion Clifton House occupied Regent

Street and the land behind it now covered by Royal York Gardens. Paul Fisher's Clifton Hill House grounds went almost to Brandon Hill and Clifton Wood House had a plot going right down to the Mardyke.

The wealthy had moved up the hill and the slump at the Hotwell was worrying the Merchant Venturers, so in 1816 they commissioned local doctor Andrew Carrick to write a report. It made dismal reading.

"In 1789 when I first became acquainted with the place, the Hotwells during summer was one of the best frequented and most crowded watering places

GET WELL SOON!

Diseases for which Bristol waters are properly prescribed are internal haemorrhages and inflammations, blood spitting, dysentary, and immoderate flux of the menses, prurulent ulcers of the viscera: hence in consumption, the dropsy, scurvy with heat, stone gravel, stranguary, the habitable gout, scorbutic rheumatism, diabetes, slow fevers, atrophy, venereal disease, cancer, gleets in both sexes, King's evil etc."

Shiercliff's Guide, **1789**.

CONSUMPTION AT THE HOTWELL

A tall gentleman with a ghastly but smiling countenance came into the room. I am really, said he, so much better and in such good spirits that I flatter myself I shall be able to dine with you. Do so, said my friend, at half past three I shall expect you. You may depend on seeing me, added the gentleman, unless something very particular happens, and accordingly, he took his leave.

At 3.30 pm a message was sent to inform him that dinner was ready; but he could not come – something very particular indeed has happened: he was under an engagement he could not break – for the servant returned and informed us that he was dead.

WORKFARE IN CLIFTON, 1787 STYLE

Vestrymen of Clifton Parish resolved "that as the poor of the parish do not frequent the service of the church but loiter in idleness and are most probably guilty of offences during the time of such service, abled bodied paupers should henceforth be required to attend prayers every Friday before receiving relief and in default of attending shall not receive the usual pay for that week. It was resolved to build a gallery for the use of paupers so that they should be compelled to attend twice on Sunday or forfeit allowances."

BUILDING MANIA

Clifton is universally allowed to be one of the most agreeable, healthy and pleasant villages in the kingdom. The delightful situation of Clifton has long since tempted several persons of large fortune to make it their principal residence, and others continuing to follow the example has occasioned the hill to be almost everywhere covered with respectable mansions, most of them built in freestone in a very elegant style and a noble Crescent is now building on a plan superior to anything of the kind. Several new streets and rows of houses are projected and are carrying forward with the utmost spirit, speed and elegance. Here also are a great number of handsome houses built purposely for letting lodgings.

Reed's New Bristol Guide, **1792**.

Clifton is situated on the top of a hill commanding a view of Bristol and its neighbourhood, conveniently elevated above the dirt and noise of the city. Here are houses, rocks, woods, town and country in one small spot; and beneath the sweetly flowing Avon, so celebrated by the poets. Indeed there can hardly be a more beautiful spot.

Humphry Davy's description of Clifton, October 1798.

So great is the spirit of building that we heard that grounds are actually taken for more than 3,000 houses.

Felix Farley's Journal **1791**.

SLUMP IN CLIFTON

The buildings here at Clifton exhibit the most melancholy appearance – you know how numerous they are, five weeks ago half the masons and carpenters were discharged; and three weeks ago all the remainder – I see not a single labourer at work – not one house in ten is covered in and I am told there is not the smallest chance of their being so before winter – part of the men enlisted – part starving.

Letter from Thomas Beddoes, 1793.

THE DISMAL SIGHT

It is to be hoped that with the restoration of peace and welcome return to opulence will lead to the gradual rise of those well-situated sublime piles which when completed will be the pride of the city and grand ornament of the country.

New Bristol Guide, **1799.**

Here too as well as at Bath is the dismal sight of streets and crescents which have never been finished, the most dolorous of ruins.

Robert Southey, 1807.

SENT THERE TO DIE

Clifton stands on a hill above the river. The stream consists of liquid mud and the banks are hideous unless the tide is full. The beauty of this scene is yearly diminishing because of quarrying. The people of Bristol seem to sell everything that can be sold; they sold their cross, their eagle [a gold lectern] and here they are selling the sublime and the beautiful by the boat-load!

I tasted the famous medicinal water which issues at the foot of these rocks; it is tepid and so completely without any medicinal flavour as to be excellent water. In cases of diabetes it can possess some virtue, for consumption, which it usually prescribed for, none whatsoever.

Several unhappy patients who had been sent there to die at a distance from home were crowding out upon the parade as if to take their last glimpse of sunshine. It was sickening to hear how thoroughly the people here regard death as a matter of trade. A sister who came with a dying brother came down to breakfast to find he had died, been laid out, put in a shroud and measured for a coffin, and the undertaker given all the orders 'to take the trouble off her hands'.

Visitors staying at one boarding house remarked on marks of injury on the staircase walls. 'That', said the landlady 'has occurred through the frequent conveyance of coffins up and down the stairs. I have had it repaired again and again, I am tired of the trouble and expense.'

Espriella Letters, **1807, by Robert Southey, in which he describes England as if he were a visiting Spaniard.**

MORE FOR FUN

The whole neighbourhood from the town to the Well as well as the hill further up called Clifton Hill are bright with lovely buildings and mansions, many of which were built to lodge the multitude of people from all places who come here in the summer months more for fun than to use the well for their health.

Bengt Ferrner, from Sweden, 1759.

MEAN STREETS

The lodging rooms above the promenade are too near the water and the exhalations from the shoals of mud, heated by the concentrated beams of the sun cannot fail to be prejudicial to the valetudinarian. Besides the streets and houses between Bristol and the Well are dirty and badly paved, and the latter meanly inhabited.

James Malcolm's *Excursions*, 1807.

AN AMERICAN VISITS MR. GOLDNEY'S GROTTO

Going through the main walk we arrived at the Door of the grotto situated under the terrass; the first object that presented itself to our view was a lion sitting; and behind in a dark cave, a lioness; the latter so much resembling life that I could hardly persuade myself to the contrary.

The form of the grotto is octangular, its roof a semicircle, a dome, in the centre atop is a round window, the diameter about 18 or 20 feet from the door in front to the mouth of the cave in which the Lioness sits. On each side to the right and left of the entrance the roof is supported by gyral pillars, covered, as its sides and roof are, with an incredible variety of shells, stones, spars, petrifications etc., etc., the mountain, nay even the bowels of the earth, to the shores of the sea, the bottom also of it seems to have been pillaged to furnish materials to adorn this curious subterranean recess.

Samuel Curwen, 1778.

in the kingdom. Scores of the first nobility were to be found there every season and such a crowd of invalids of all ranks resorted to the waters that it was often difficult to provide them with lodgings.

"Three extensive taverns were constantly full, and two spacious ballrooms were profitably kept open. There was a well attended ball, public breakfasts and a promenade every week and often twice a week. The Pump Room was all day long the resort of invalids, who left with the keeper of the well many hundreds a year in voluntary donations and from 12 to 2 was generally so crowded that there was often some difficulty in getting up to drink the water. The walk adjoining was in the meantime filled with fashionable company, . . . the Downs and all the avenues to the Hotwells were filled with strings of carriages, and with parties on horseback and on foot.

"Then in 1816 there was the silence of the grave, to which it seems the inlet. Not a carriage to be seen once an hour, and scarcely more frequently does a solitary invalid approach the neglected spring . . . Not one tenth of the visitors of rank and fortune, and of invalids a still smaller proportion, resorted to the place and the letters of lodgings became almost universally bankrupt in a few years.

"From that day the Hot Well became a fountain sealed to the lips of everyone but the actually moribund, the fame of the place began rapidly to decline. None who drank of the Lethean waters were thenceforth found to recover because none did drink of it but such as were past recovery. It was now one uniform black list of disappointment and death and in the course of a very few years it became all over the kingdom a source of horror and despair, instead of joy and confidence, to be ordered to the Hot Well, from whose bourne no traveller returned."

19. The notorious poet-milkmaid, Ann Yearsley who quarrelled with her patron Hannah More and set up a library in the Colonnade.

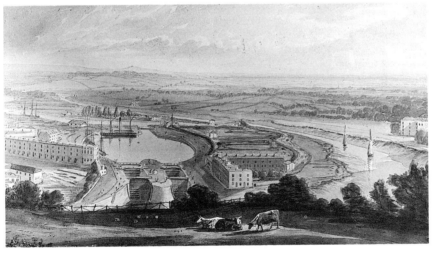

20. *Above*: This 1850 lithograph shows Clifton's spectacular growth, with the Suspension Bridge still unfinished.

21. The Cumberland Basin before Brunel's improvements: a surprisingly rural view from Rownham Hill by Samuel Jackson c.1825.

AVON WATERS.

A Song, written for this Work, by Joseph H. Butler.

Air, ".Bonny Doon."

Thou bonny stream of Avon fair,
 For ever roll thy silver tide!
Young Spring's first flowers shall linger there,
 Along thy banks of verdant pride.
And there the *stock-dove's* sweetest note
 Shall plaintive sound thy woods among;
And Summer breezes softly float
 Upon thy* classic breast of song!

'Twas on thy banks of early bloom
 Unfolded life's young blossom;
Clear shone my sky from winter's gloom,
 And free from woe my bosom.—
And there young love first lisp'd the name
 Of her I lov'd so dearly;
Oft to thy banks we fondly came,
 On Summer's evening early.

There last I saw her bright blue eye
 That beamed with love so tender;
And there with many a heart-felt sigh,
 Our love was torn asunder.
Dark are her eyes, and cold her clay;
 My star is set for ever!—
Where does thy gentle spirit stray?
 May we not meet?—No! never!

Green is the sod that wraps thy grave
 Thou young and peerless blossom;
Nor prayer nor tear avail'd to save
 This idol of my bosom.
Then flow thy waters, Avon flow,
 For ever clear and brightly;
And on my Mary's breast of snow
 Thou verdant sod lie lightly!

Bristol, Dec. 1848.

* An allusion to Shakspeare's birthplace.

From Morgan's New Picture of Clifton.

THIS BUILDING
ORIGINALLY AN HOTEL AND ASSEMBLY ROOM
WAS DESIGNED BY
FRANCIS HOWARD GREENWAY
1777—1837

HE BECAME KNOWN AS
THE FATHER OF AUSTRALIAN ARCHITECTURE
FOR HIS LATER WORK IN THAT CONTINENT

ERECTED BY THE AUSTRALIAN HIGH COMMISSION
AND THE CLIFTON AND HOTWELLS IMPROVEMENT SOCIETY 1977

22. & 23. Francis Greenway's Assembly Rooms in The Mall, Clifton. Greenway was later deported to Australia for fraud and forgery.

24. The interior of the Assembly Rooms, as seen by Hotwells artist, Rolinda Sharples, 1817–1820.

25. The artist's self portrait.

33

26. A sketching party in Nightingale Valley, Leigh Woods, by Samuel Jackson c. 1825.

27. Artists Samuel Jackson and Francis Danby at Number 1, Cambridge Place (now 8 Canynge Square) in 1855.

28. Elegant Clifton: Royal York Crescent about 1850 (lithograph by W.L. Walton).

29. Boyce's Buildings as they originally looked, before being truncated by the building of Merchant's Road.

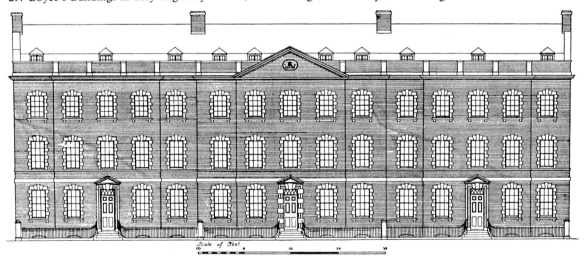

FIGURE 28
Boyce's Buildings, Clifton. Elevation

36

SOME TERRIBLE POEMS ABOUT CLIFTON

Clifton, sweet village! now demands the lay,
The lov'd retreat of all the rich and gay;
The darling spot which pining maidens seek
To give Health's roses to the pallid cheek.
Warm from its font the holy water pours,
And lures the sick to Clifton's neighbouring bowers.

Thomas Chatterton, 1769.

High on a hill with beauteous structures spread
Delightful Clifton rears its rural head,
And looks with pleasure on the vales below,
Where towns are planted and where rivers flow.

William Heard, 1778.

"Hail Clifton! Where Nature Elegance and Art divine,
Continue where town and country's charms united shine.
Here smiling crescents rise in grand array
And stately buildings deck the summit gay."

John Antrobus, 1834.

Hail Clifton scenes! to me your charms impart,
They raise my senses – captivate my heart.
For whilst I these divine mementoes scan,
I smite my breast, and cry "Lord, what is man?"

John Morgan, Bristol bookseller, 1851.

Mansions in terrac'd lines from ledge to ledge
Of shrub-clad rocks creep down to Avon's edge;
On their rugged and precipitious face,
Beetling o'er th'abyss hangs Windsor Terrace,
And sees with ruin t'its neighbours menace.
A horse to carriage yok'd once took the leap.*
Brunel's Twin Follies next appear,
Monsters doomed a suspended bridge to bear.
* Refers to a Miss Richmond "lured by botanic spell" who fell to her death
from the end of Windsor Terrace – "around this cliff let all bid fences rise!"

From the Poetic Guide to Clifton, *1859.*

Clifton, in vain thy varied scenes invite –
The mossy bank, dim glade, and dizzy height,
The sheep that starting from the tufted thyme
Untune the distant churches' mellow chime.

Walter Savage Landor: 'An English Scene.'

30. Clifton in 1850.

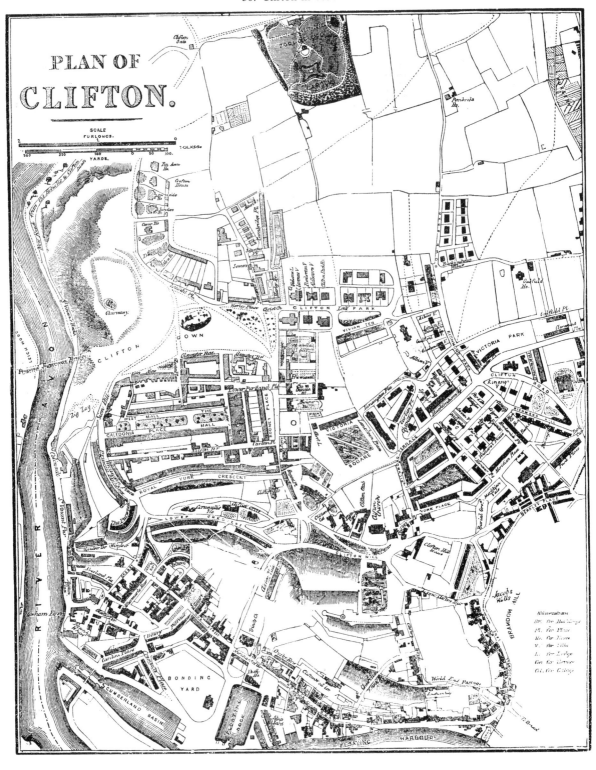

"Clifton and its Advantages"

Clifton in the first three or four decades of the nineteenth century was plainly an interesting and lively place, quite separate from the city – it officially became part of Bristol only in 1835. From a population of 4,457 in the first census of 1801, the number of inhabitants rose to 12,032 by 1831.

Because of the constant comings and goings, it was by no means dull: the artistic and literary set of Bristol, Southey, Lovell Beddoes, the Edgeworths, Hannah More, Francis Danby and the Bristol school of artists all congregated in Clifton, to find kindred spirits.

But the village lacked a social focus. There was the Clifton Assembly Rooms, where subscription balls were held in the winter, and the York Hotel in Gloucester Place, but most entertainment had to take place in private houses.

Clifton then was still thought of as very much an outdoor place where you went for walks or rides, botanised, sketched (as Brunel did on his first recuperative visit in 1829), went picnicking and so on. There were the Clifton Races on the Downs, by Sea Walls, where there had been impromptu races as early as 1758. The races by Regency times were two day events which would attract entrants from all over the country, to race for the famous Bristol Cup, now in the possession of the Merchant Venturers. But in winter there was little to do.

In the 1830s this lack led to the formation of two institutions which were to play an important part in the social life of Clifton – the Zoo and the Victoria Rooms.

The Zoo was established in 1835 when capital of £7,500 was raised in £25 shares – Brunel and W.D. and H.O. Wills were subscribers. A site of 12 acres, by the Clifton turnpike house, was bought and turned into gardens.

It opened on July 11th, 1836, and became the focus of outdoor entertainments for Clifton. The original aim was to promote zoology, arboriculture and horticulture; it was to be a scientific institute devoted to popular culture. But to finance it, income came from fetes, fireworks, fairs, concerts, croquet and archery tournaments. In 1844 half the Zoo's income came from these events, and this was a pattern for most of the nineteenth century.

Later on there were brass band concerts in the 1850s, gymnastic displays, balloon ascents; in 1855 Master Drouet the unrivalled Lilliputian clog dancer, and Signor Gomez the Modern Samson gave an exhibition of their powers, and there were flower shows, acrobats, jugglers, tightrope dancers, and the lake was used for launching lifeboats. Bicycle races were held – W.G. Grace won in 1866 – and a colossal reproduction of the siege and capture of Delhi was once built there.

The point was that these events, being held in Clifton, were thus made respectable. Of course similar entertainment was available in Bristol, but you now didn't have to leave Clifton to see it.

The Victoria Rooms, one of Clifton's finest public buildings, was established for much the same reason: a better class of person could be entertained there – and at higher ticket prices.

The Victoria Rooms foundation stone was laid in 1838 in a district where there were formerly squalid cottages, and Conservatives raised £25,000, a large sum then, for a building that would definitely raise the tone of Clifton. They employed Charles Dyer as architect and must have been well pleased with the handsome neo-classical results, and the enclosed grass lawn and gravel path in front.

The frontage was designed so that carriages could drive in one side and out of the other, and there was a hall at the back where servants could wait for their masters.

The first public meeting at the Victoria Rooms was of the Royal Agricultural Society; other early users were the Bristol Madrigal Society, whose Ladies' Night was one of the social events of the year.

The Madrigal Society was then all male (it remained so until 1946) but once a year the mothers and sisters and wives and daughters were invited to be the audience at an evening of glees, rounds and madrigals, with refreshments. It was so popular that tickets had to be rationed – 1,300 people attended in 1845 – and there was usually trouble with gate-crashers.

Dressmakers were busy months in advance and displayed their creations in their windows, and the queue of carriages in the 1840s was said to stretch for nearly a mile.

The Rooms were used for recitals, concerts,

31. Going to the races: a Frith-like study by Rolinda Sharples of the crowds at Clifton Races on the Downs.

lectures and demonstrations, on anything from mesmerism to the Pope; Jenny Lind sang there in 1847 and Adelina Patti in 1862. Dickens came with his theatre company, in 1851, to perform a comedy *Not So Bad As We Seem*. Every seat was sold out days before and the performances had to be repeated two days later.

Dickens came again in 1866 and read excerpts from *Nicholas Nickleby*, *Pickwick Papers* and *David Copperfield*. One man who attended treasured all his life a shilling given to him when he fetched the famous man a glass of water.

Later visitors were to be Oscar Wilde who lectured on aesthetics, well before he was disgraced, naturally; Maskelyn and Cook brought magic shows, Lola Montez sang.

Physically, before 1850, Clifton was much smaller and still quite rural: there were virtually no houses beyond Canynge Square, Pembroke Road was yet

to be built on, and fields stretched between it and Whiteladies Road, which was developed only on the Clifton side; Tyndall's parkland was the far boundary of Queen's Road.

The present street names reflect old fields or old history: Victoria Street was so named in 1830 – before that it was Nelson Street, after the hero of Trafalgar. Victoria Square, named after the queen's accession, was originally Ferney Close. The Litfields or lead fields became Litfield Place, Cecil's lead fields became Cecil Road. Honeypen Hill, where the pigs were penned, was a quarry now covered by Park Place and Richmond Hill. In 1866, cattle still grazed on the land now occupied by Royal York Villas. The Zig Zag opened in 1829, and was improved in 1849.

One field, at the junction of Oakfield Road and Pembroke Road long survived before it became Hanbury Road South in 1876; by about 1860 the

32. The Victoria Rooms in 1869 long before the fountain was added.

33. & 34. Charles Dickens and Oscar Wilde were popular performers.

41

whole agricultural aspect of the parish and of the older throughfares had been transformed and after the opening of Clifton College the few remaining plots speedily disappeared.

Garaway and Mayes, the eighteenth century nursery firm in the 1850s had land leading into three fields that stretched from Whiteladies Road to Pembroke Road. "Respectable pedestrians at proper hours are allowed to go through from the high road into the fields behind, merely by asking at their counting house, in the summer months."

The bad state of the roads has already been mentioned; things gradually improved when John Loudon McAdam came to live at 6, Sion Hill in 1815. A plaque at 23 Berkeley Square records that he lived there, too – from 1805 to 1808. His great contribution was the idea that roads should be built up, not dug out, and that six to ten inches of finely broken stone should be laid to provide a surface which would not break up under the weight of carriages.

But he could only improve roads adopted by Bristol Corporation and most in Clifton, apart from the turnpike, were private roads. So ironically, though he lived there, complaints about Clifton roads went on and on – and still do.

But he did do some work in the area, altering the inclines to build new roads on Blackboy Hill, Rownham Hill and Richmond Terrace and he designed the new Clifton turnpike road over the Downs and past the Zoo.

Clifton was still awkward to get to because a road through Victoria Square was not opened until 1858: to get to the Mall, carriages had to go either up Clifton Hill and along through Regent Street, or come from the top of the Downs on the turnpike road, or from the Hotwell Road via Granby Hill.

One famous short cut was from Victoria Square into Boyce's Avenue, through a gate: it was however a private right of way owned by the eccentric William Mathias, whose uncle had bought Boyce's Buildings in 1828.

The trespassers drove him mad: he built walls, he built gates, and they were regularly torn down and the police were called. Complaints about his "blockade" crowded the letters columns of the *Clifton Chronicle*. In the end there was a famous court case, when Mathias was charged with assaulting a woman who lifted a perambulator over his gate. He was found not guilty and the arguments finally ended when Merchants Road was opened in 1858,

and traffic could get through to the heart of Clifton that way.

(Mathias, a truly Dickensian eccentric, became obsessed with litigation and spent thousands of pounds on it. He was a property speculator who lived in Albemarle Row, and owned houses in Royal York Crescent: he built Pharmacy Arch and the shops on the side of Boyce's Buildings. He was much criticised for leaving houses void, so that they were stripped of their lead. He left two houses in Boyce's Buildings empty for seven years, and one of the best houses in Royal York Crescent for 12 years, and in 1873 at the age of 92 he was committed to prison for contempt of the Court of Chancery)

But as Clifton was growing in size and importance, Hotwells gently and sadly declined.

The Hotwell itself now had rivals: as well as the Tennis Court House spring, still going strong in the 1820s with "hot and cold baths and a neat pump room in the house and a small colonnade before the door" there were other sources, at the site of the Spring Gardens pub in the Hotwell Road, at Richmond Hill, and there were two more in Buckingham Place and Whiteladies Road. A really serious rival, because it was at the top of the hill in a fashionable area, was the Sion Spring.

This was discovered in the 1780s when a bore was made 250 feet into the rock; the spring produced 33,560 gallons a day, a bath house (the much altered Zig Zag bar building next to St. Vincent's Rocks Hotel) was built with a spacious pump room 50 ft by 30 ft, a subscription room for readers of newspapers, and a garden for the reception of company.

The Sion Spring never attracted a great store of company as did the Hotwell in its heyday, and the pump room was soon turned into a library and reading room. But the plentiful supply of water meant that houses nearby could have a supply delivered into cisterns in their cellars – the iron traps in the pavement are still visible – and in the 1840s, 400 houses were supplied by this spring. There was even an idea of giving Richmond Terrace residents central heating via their hot spring nearby.

All these sources of water were bought up when Bristol Waterworks were formed in 1846.

But a few still looked to the Hotwell for a cure. The old Hotwell House was pulled down in 1822, but in 1850 an engineer, James Bolton, took over the subsequent building, and set out to revive the spa, with a new suite of baths. He also sold souvenirs and bottled mineral water drinks made

RACES ON THE DOWNS

"Clifton Races began today; the company was more brilliant and numerous than we ever recollect and the appearance of the grandstand and the long line of carriages formed a ludicrous comment on the supposed distress of the times."

Bristol Gazette, 1830.

THE YORK HOTEL, SION PLACE

This has an elegant Ballroom with a good organ and commands a picturesque view of Leigh Woods and the Downs. The whole building is a capital hotel, handsomely fitted up and extremely well calculated for parties who arrive here or make excursions for a few days to this delightful spot. It is kept by William Evans and is situated in Gloucester Place.

Matthews Guide, 1793–4.

HOLIER THAN THOU

An immense multitude of spectators of all ranks and descriptions assembled and the scene wore a most appealing character. The doors opened at 10.30 am for holders of 4s. tickets. Afterwards the Lord Bishop and the Dean together with many of the clergy partook of a capital dinner at the Clifton Hotel during and after which the utmost harmony and gentlemanly deportment prevailed.

Felix Farley's Journal on the consecration of the rebuilt parish church of St. Andrew, 1822.

NO HOPE OF A CURE

Every candid practitioner will acknowledge that the Spa has rarely been resorted to in consumptive cases till the patient has sunk beyond the reach of curative treatment. Sent here as a forlorn hope when all professional advice has been exhausted, how many gentle victims to phthisis have reached the fount, merely to expend whatever yet lingered of the vis vitae. They have in truth bowed to taste the wave and died. To cure such patients as have from time to time been brought there in the most deplorable state of the malady would have demanded a miracle.

Herapath's handbook for Visitors to the Hotwell, 1830.

A HEALING PROSPECT

I have to thank my friends for one of the most beautiful as well as comfortable rooms you could desire. I look from my window upon the Avon and its wooded and rocky bounds – the trees yet green. A vessel is sailing down and here comes a steamer (Irish I suppose). I have in my view the end of the Cliff on my right and on my left a wide and varied prospect over Bristol as far as the eye can reach. Clifton was always a favourite place with me. I have more strength and more spirits since my arrival in this place.

George Crabbe, who visited Clifton in 1831.

THE POOR MAN AT HIS GATE

Clifton church is not to any extent the church of the parishioners; the rich and the non-resident occupy the reserved seats and those few that are nominally free are filled with powdered footmen. It is not the church of a poor man, he has no business there in that atmosphere of eau de Cologne, bouquet de la Reine, where the glitter of gilt-edged prayer books and the rustle of brocades present sounds and sights extraordinary to humble comprehension. Dowagers young and old finely clad, nodding plumes and flowing dresses swept on and still the expectants stood by the porch.

John Leech, The Churchgoer, on St. Andrew's Parish Church Clifton in the 1840s.

MUGGINGS IN CLIFTON

Gentlemen who transparished themselves to Clifton are at risk. The roads leading to Clifton are so infested at night with desperadoes that few gentlemen think it safe to walk about alone or unarmed.

Bristol Journal, 1819.

35. & 36. How the architect envisaged the Royal Promenade, with the gardens as originally planned. This was the first terrace to be built in Victoria Square in the late 1830s. The cricketer, W.G. Grace was to be a later resident, living at Number 16.

37. Gas lighting comes to Clifton: Victoria Square in the 1850s.

with Hotwell water, Hotwell toothpowder, and he even peddled boomerangs.

The poor old Hotwell spa itself lingered on until 1867 when the Pump Room was demolished. After complaints, the pump was enclosed and piped to a small cave in the rock so that the public could drink the water, free.

In any case the water cure was then long discounted: it was dimly realised that public health now depended on a healthy environment and this was what Clifton could provide. Clifton prided itself on its health statistics, though they were inconveniently spoiled by the fact the Clifton Parish, in its Poor Law responsibilities, included some slum areas of Bristol.

Yet it is true that when a cholera epidemic hit Bristol in 1832, Clifton escaped. John King, the surgeon who lived at 26, The Mall reported: "The cholera is much abated in this parish; it has not yet found its way up the hill and scarcely beyond the dirty purlieus of Lime Kiln Lane and the worst courts in the Hotwell Road, nor has it attacked a single individual above the lowest class." So that was all right.

In Clifton, Dr. William Budd the great public health pioneer was already aware how diseases spread; he tracked down an outbreak of typhoid in 1847 to an infected water supply in Richmond Terrace and by 1856 he was working on his theory that tuberculosis was infectious and caused by a specific germ – and that the last place to go for your health was a pump room where consumptives were taking the waters, and eating and drinking together.

Being on the hill at least meant sewage in cesspits and open sewers drained away downwards, to the poorer areas below – residents on the heights could breathe purer air, above the industrial pollution of the city centre. But in 1844, there were still only 400 houses in Clifton with piped water; a stinking gutter ran down Whiteladies Road, and several open sewers met at Clifton Gate. Most houses had cesspits, since there was no sanitary authority to provide mains drainage and in summer the stench must have been unbearable.

In the damning 1844 report on public health in Bristol, the inspectors found: "In a field in front of west Clifton Terrace (now Alma Road) the sewage escapes over a large space. A resident at Vittoria Place said that it was impossible to support the stench at night. Oakfield Road was a perfect quagmire. At the back of Park Place a filthy crossroad and a market garden the stench of which was much complained of." At this time, nightsoil was still collected for fertiliser.

Ill-health in the now poor Hotwells district was from 1812 on being dealt with at the Clifton Dispensary in Dowry Square. It was founded by Thomas Whippie at his own expense and ran on a subscription system, whereby the wealthy who gave donations were given a proportionate number of tickets which they gave out to the deserving poor who came to ask for them. Each ticket entitled the holder to medical attention.

As the visitors never came to the Hotwell in such great numbers as before, all the landlords and landladies who had made a living by letting lodgings in the big Georgian houses went bankrupt or sold up. The big elegant houses were turned into tenements for poor families working on the docks; and new artisan dwellings were built as infilling, or in mean little courts one house wide, off the Hotwell Road. The Long Room, scene of so much elegance, became a school in 1812 and remained so until 1963 when it was demolished to build the Cumberland Basin flyover.

But the Gorge itself was still a great attraction to sightseers and artists, and went on inspiring more terrible poetry, though the quarrying and exploitation of the woods was beginning to leave great raw gaps and scars on the landscape.

In 1842 there was a protest at the destruction of the natural beauty of Leigh Woods, when a portion of the British Camp was converted into a potato garden, and the woods let as a rabbit warren, beauty spots were fenced off, and the river bank was blasted away. A newspaper editorial thundered "Of the unintelligent, unscrupulous and merely mercenary and vulgar character of the general invasion of which this fine scenery has long been a victim, there can be in every generous and feeling mind but one opinion."

The devastation of the riverside went on; though Blackrock Quarry was closed in 1868, permission was given for another on the Somerset side leaving what Latimer called another hideous gash. The Downs area too was full of quarries: one excavated in 1848 disclosed bones of hyenas, bear, rhino, hippo and wild boar. The area behind Worrall Road was quarried, and land in front of Belgrave Road, and these holes were only filled up when materials excavated for Cumberland Basin lock were ferried up to the Downs by a special tramway built to

OBSERVATORY, CLIFTON.

To the Ladies and Gentlemen visiting the romantic Scenery of Clifton, the Proprietor takes the liberty of recommending the Observatory to their notice, as being by far the most eligible point to obtain a clear idea of the locality and beauty of the place, independent of the amusement afforded by the various Instruments.

ADMISSION—One Shilling ; Juniors under 12 years, Sixpence each.

Subscribers 10s. 6d. per Annum ; 5s. per Month includes the use of the Instruments by Day, the Cave, &c.

38. & 39. Clifton grew in popularity, while Hotwells fought back in vain: James Bolton's revival of the Hotwells baths was short-lived in the 1860s.

MODERN YOUTH

We have one of the most disorderly set of youths in England; stones are continually thrown by boys in our streets, and many lives have been lost, five at least in Clifton parish. Ornamental plantations are constantly injured and the branches carried away for firewood. Young thieves assemble at each end of Park Street, professedly to drag the streets [hold the carriage horses] but really for worse purposes. If police complain they are assaulted by indecent language revolting to all, especially to females.

A Clifton magistrate, 1856.

WORDS FAIL HIM

Here indeed it may truly be said that the visitor has arrived at one of nature's loveliest spots for the scenery from and about the Observatory is highly romantic and picturesque with immense declivities of rocks on the north east side of the Avon. The man of taste could ever gaze upon it with rapture and astonishment. (As many accidents have occurred here by persons falling over, strangers are cautioned against going too near the brink of this immense precipice). The scene is too variegated, too immense, too resplendent a character to receive any just delineation either from the pencil of the artist or the inspiration of the poet.

Morgan's Guide **1851.**

THE SOCIAL WHIRL

We are glad to perceive that Lady Horatia Webbe Weston and Lady Ida Waldegrave have taken No. 16 Caledonia Place for a short time. We hope these ladies, who are members of the illustrious house of Waldegrave, and the many other nobility who are wintering among us may find the fashionable watering places of Clifton sufficiently agreeable to think of making it their permanent residence. [A modern Waldegrave, William, the MP for Bristol West, lived for a time in what was in 1857 considered a slum – Wellington Terrace.]

Clifton Chronicle, **June 1852.**

A FATAL FALL

A young lady, Miss Martha W--- was observed one morning sitting on a dangerous projection of a crag above the Giant's Cave. Being warned of her peril she withdrew but must have returned, for she was seen falling through the air from 300 feet. She stretched out her hands and tried to grasp the ivy and then lay at the bottom a shapeless and inanimate mass.

Report of an accident at the Gorge, October 1847.

CHARITY BEGINS AT HOTWELLS

Dinner for the Old People of Clifton with roast beef, bread, plum pudding was served at 24 tables for 320 guests in the long disused ballroom at the Hotwells. The Entertainment was for poor people over 60 of good character. The ballroom was decorated with flowers, flags and scriptural texts. Though poor, they were cleanly dressed, and each was given packet of tea and sugar and a fly home if too feeble to walk.

Clifton Chronicle, **January 13th, 1858.**

AN UNFASHIONABLE WEDDING, 1852

We hear of a lady of good family and enjoying a fortune in her own right marrying a man of the humblest class, with a job holding horses of carriages going down Park Street. The Lady was a district visitor and called upon the young man's mother. The vicar of Christchurch refused to marry them so they got married at Wells with no bridesmaids, no best man, no cards, and they took up residence in a locality that was in the last century a fashionable part, Hotwells. He was 17 or 18, she verging on 30. [This spiteful report was denied by the lady; she corrected all the claims in a letter to the editor, who rebuked her for daring to dispute the facts!]

Clifton Chronicle.

convey it.

As Clifton's housing development gradually spread over the fields and onto the Downs, the place began to take on a firmer identity. There were Clifton ways of doing things.

This was particularly true of the church. Originally religion centred on the old parish church of St. Andrew, which thanks to society at the Hotwell, became fashionable in the eighteenth century. Wesley preached there in 1754 and wrote "seeing many of the rich of Clifton Church, my heart was pained for them and was earnestly desirous that some even of them might enter into the Kingdom of Heaven".

By the turn of the nineteenth century the church was too small, and it was rebuilt in 1822, the capital being raised by renting pews or granting them in perpetuity to those who contributed a certain sum. Since the new church held 2,000 people, a lot of money was involved.

For status-loving Cliftonians, your own pew was a must – one went for auction in 1836 at £190. One person owned 13 pews and rented them out, and seats were often sold with houses, being mentioned in house particulars. "Pew mongering" was still going strong in 1873 when "a pew in the parish church, best situation facing the pulpit, £88" was advertised.

Private pews caused ill feeling because they kept out visitors and servants (there was a plan to build a gallery for them) and in the end those against it gave their pews up, and church officials eventually bought most of them up for £3,000.

By 1884, 700 out of 2,000 sittings were free but even in 1940 there was still one proprietory pew left. "I know of nothing more calculated to send men Romewards than this scandal," said one enraged member of the congregation.

Since it was obvious there would never be enough seats for visitors and residents, let alone their servants, another new church had to be built and in 1841, Christ Church was consecrated. It cost £10,500, and was enlarged in 1859, and side aisles added in 1885.

Clifton also began to acquire the utilities. Some of the dusty roads were watered by private subscription, but by 1861, the Corporation had taken over the watering of eight miles of Clifton's pre-tarmac roads. Dust was a permanent source of complaint in dry weather, as was mud in wet weather: it meant a loss for traders, because people would not shop in dusty streets, and shopowners had to water the road themselves.

There were a few gas street lamps in Clifton by 1824, after the formation of the Bristol and Clifton Gas Company the year before. (The Company was forbidden to use coal at first, and had to rely on oil; its ruined works in Anchor Road can still be seen) Soon the entire suburb was lit by gas and gas lighting survives in Canynge Square to this day. In 1847 the Victoria Rooms had installed three gas lamps reckoned to have 60 candlepower.

Domestic lighting by gas also came surprisingly early. In 1841 a builder offered to install piping in the new houses in West Mall "under the supposition that tenants may be influenced to use gas."

Until 1846 Clifton had no official post office, merely a receiving house just beyond Saville Place, in a pastry cook's shop. But in 1846 the Chamber of Commerce backed Clifton residents "including peers, magistrates, solicitors, doctors" in asking for the status of the office to be raised. It was a measure of Clifton's social status that it got a branch, on the site of the now abandoned Post Office in Regent Street that very year, with Mr W. Wrighton as superintendent. (The floor above was let to Mrs Toplis and Mr Huxtable for dancing and music classes)

Clifton also was given a police station early on; before 1835, the military dealt with disorder, but in 1836 the police station on Brandon Hill was set up with one Inspector, six sergeants and 53 constables with fixed beats and a rota of day and night patrols. The Inspector got £1.10s a week, the sergeants £1. 4s. 6d, and the constables 16s.

Each got cape, greatcoat, frock coat, trousers, boots, top hat, stock, button brushes, rattle and lamp. Fifty cutlasses and 24 pairs of handcuffs were kept at the station. One of the Rules read: "It is forbidden to enter into conversation with female servants or to walk or to converse with comrades." Police could be hired for private functions and did duties at the Victoria Rooms and the Bristol races. They were tipped for mundane services like catching a pig.

Another sign of a settled community was its own newspaper, the *Clifton Chronicle*, which started in November 1850 to list all the social events, and the arrivals and departures of visitors: it published a complete street directory of all residents, every week. It was to the modern researcher a nightmarish slab of print, until 1891 without headlines, with

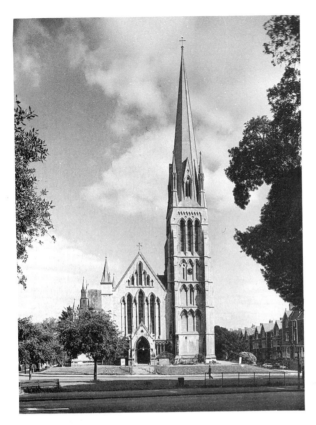

40. Christ Church as it looks today.

41. Still rural Clifton showing the old St. Andrew's Church which was demolished in 1822 and rebuilt (engraving by J. Skelton).

42. The Royal West of England Academy as originally built in 1858, with the triumphal double staircase. The mother of the artist, Rolinda Sharples contributed to the building costs.

A FASHIONABLE WEDDING AT CHRISTCHURCH, 1859

The bride wore a dress of ruched white taffeta glace with double skirt ornaments with tulle illusion and ruches of taffeta; high bodice, the sleeves very wide and open, trimmed with ruches of taffeta, lined with silk and edged with quilled ribbon; full illusion sleeves under. An elegant blonde veil entirely covered the whole dress.

Clifton Chronicle.

A SINGULAR COINCIDENCE

Last week Fanny Harris, a cook, fell over the steps near Royal York Crescent and severely fractured her ancle (sic). She was taken to the Infirmary by Clifton Police. A sister of the unfortunate woman was apprised of the occurence and while leaving her house she fell down the stairs and fractured her leg.

Clifton Chronicle, 1863.

THE SERVANT PROBLEM

We often complain that servants are pert and disrespectful in their manner and language but is there not often a cause in ourselves? By petulance or sharpness of tone, we chafe the spirits of those under us and then complain of the irritability which we engendered. It is unjust to charge them with dishonesty upon light grounds. I would caution employers against hasty dismissal.
Advice to servants: I very much fear that servants who dress above their station want to appear what they are not.

Addresses by the Rev S.A. Walker, 1860.

A DARING BURGLARY

The premises of Mr Henry Pearce, proprietor of the Sion Spring Baths at the top of the Zig-Zag were burglarised, entered and robbed. The thieves got first on to the top of an adjacent house, and having helped themselves to some dozen boxes of cigars, many of them of expensive description, a cameo brooch, three snuff boxes and a lot of fancy pebble and agate brooches set in silver, to the value of about £13, they decamped. In order to get out they placed a short ladder on a table which stood underneath the skylight and having ascended the roof once more made their way to the street and then set off in the direction of the Hotwells.

Clifton Chronicle, **May 29th, 1861.**

POVERTY IN CLIFTON

I do not speak of poverty in the notoriously poor district of the Hotwells. I speak of Clifton proper where the contrast between the commodious houses and fine shops of the upper and middle classes and the crampt ill-ventilated dwellings of the working and petty tradesman which mingle with them, is pitifully apparent.
Wellington Place opposite Princes Buildings is shabby and decayed. Almost every family house is let out in several divisions, a whole family occupying the underground kitchen with perhaps a single garret in addition for high rent of 4s. a week. Waterloo Place is equally squalid and the court which winds from it to the Mall buildings is unliveable. These three sets of houses form the main accommodation for the Clifton work people and are far from cheap, Miles' Court has dark unfurnished rooms for 2s.3d. a week.

Letter to *Clifton Chronicle*, **1857.**

A lady named Andrews and a daughter reside at Sion Hill where until recently, the mother kept a lodging house. Some time ago the furniture was sold by auction and the house was completely stripped of everything in it except one or two old chairs which the poor woman had been obliged to use as a bed. To crown their misfortunes the daughter on Saturday night was delivered of twins ... I hope the benevolent of Clifton will give assistance.

Letter to the *Western Daily Press*, **1864.**

news, local, national and foreign, court reports, opinion, observation, fiction and gossip, all mixed up together, advertisements on the front page and ultra conservative politics throughout.

The *Chronicle* reflected the snobbery of the Clifton social scene, which by the late 1850s was riven by various factions.

Rival groups set up private subscription balls at the Assembly Rooms and the Victoria Rooms. To prevent anyone and everyone coming, people had to apply for tickets in advance from a committee, and in 1860 the well-born William Poole King who lived at one of the best addresses in Clifton, 1, Rodney Place, was refused a ticket by the son of a London undertaker.

This caused heated correspondence from both sides in the *Bristol Mirror* and the ensuing row was said to have "broken up Clifton society" and some families actually moved house because of it!

The slanging matches came down to the level of personal abuse: the patroness of one of the Victoria Rooms balls caused much ill-feeling by refusing to forward tickets of admission to a lady until she produced her marriage certificate. Her response to this was that she would do so as soon as the patroness produced specimens of the weekly washing bills she used to forward to her customers. . . .

After this, not surprisingly, subscription balls went out of fashion, and only private ones were held from then on.

There was by then a geographical reason for Clifton's sense of exclusivity. The importance of the Downs to Bristol was finally recognised in 1861 when the Merchant Venturers handed them over to the Corporation, and the area was established as a green lung for the city. No more building was to be allowed – before then, houses had been built on the Downs willy nilly without permission.

The preservation of the Downs had an immediate effect on Clifton, for they formed a natural boundary and cut Clifton off into an exclusive, defined area that could not grow any larger. Land values shot up accordingly and the upwardly mobile were pierced with an ambition to live there.

So Clifton gradually became more and more insular and snobbish. A dreadful respectability took over, and an obsession with social niceties, precedence, etiquette, and appearances. Clifton was getting dull and smug. It needed shaking up and the unlikely agent was a new school, Clifton College.

43. – 45. Grand houses, crescents and terraces: Clifton Hill House, home of the writer John Addington Symonds; The Paragon with sweeping views; and Windsor Terrace, which bankrupted its builder, William Watts. Hannah More, writer and philanthropist, lived at Number 4.

CLIFTON IN 1880.

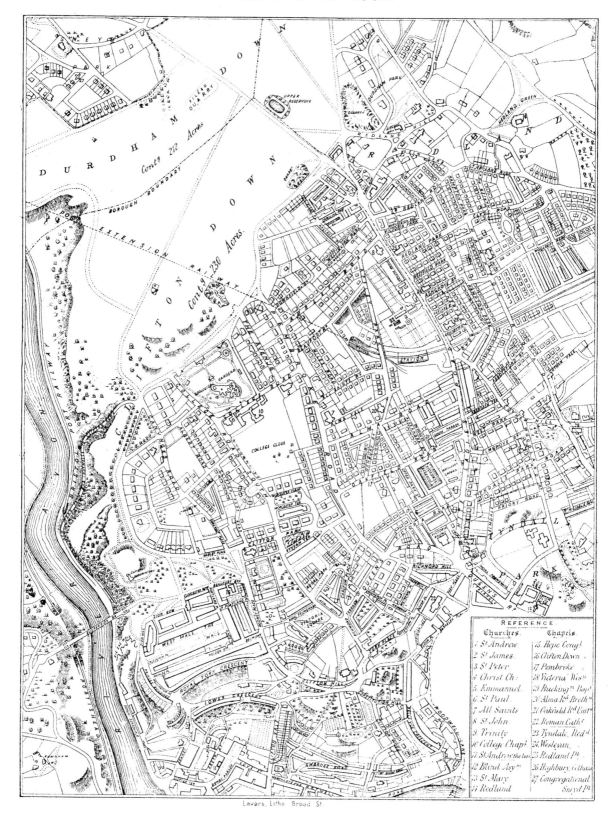

REFERENCE

Churches	Chapels
1. St Andrew.	15. Hope Congl.
2. St James.	16. Clifton Down
3. St Peter.	17. Pembroke
4. Christ Ch.	18. Victoria Wesn
5. Emmanuel.	19. Buckingm Bapt
6. St Paul.	20. Alma Rd Brethn
7. All Saints	21. Oakfield Rd Unit
8. St John.	22. Roman Cathc
9. Trinity	23. Tyndale, Red.d
10. College Chapl	24. Wesleyan,
11. St Andrew the less	25. Redland Pk
12. Blind Asym	26. Highbury, Cotham
13. St Mary.	27. Congregational
14. Redland	Snuyd Pk

Lavars, Litho Broad St.

"A somewhat sluggish social condition"

Two new arrivals in Clifton were to change the place radically: one was the Suspension Bridge which in 1864 gave Clifton a new tourist attraction and the other was Clifton College.

It was not just the arrival of a serious educational institution, run in the great Rugby tradition, that was important, though this was sorely needed. Clifton was full of minor private academies, and Cliftonians were jealous of the public schools at Marlborough and Cheltenham.

The school also had great social impact. Just as Clifton was getting stuffy, clique-ridden and snobbish, the school and its young clergyman-headmaster John Percival brought a mental breath of fresh air. The local MP, Lewis Fry, said that he "introduced into our somewhat sluggish social condition a life and energy which has been of inestimable value."

The Clifton masters stimulated intellectual debate and had new and challenging ideas to talk over at Clifton dinner parties, for the staff were radicals and liberals, and in conservative Clifton terms quite daring: housemaster George Wollaston decorated his drawing room at his house in College Road with a black carpet and a black ceiling, always dressed for dinner, and wore a velvet collar on his coat.

The school also brought new people into Clifton, for one of the great attractions for parents who did not want their sons to board was that day boys were encouraged. Percival believed that the best education could be obtained by a boy who lived in a good home, and attended a good school near his home.

So there was a physical impact too: as well as the new school buildings, all the fields nearby were quickly built upon and many of the large and comfortable new houses were rented by parents who came to live in Clifton while their sons were educated. The Newbolt family moved to 6, Worcester Crescent while Henry of 'Play up, play up and play the game' fame and his brother Francis attended Clifton.

Daughters benefitted too, for the establishment of a fine school for boys inevitably led to a cry for the same kind of education for girls, and John Percival was behind the founding of Clifton High School and sent his daughter Bessie there when it opened in 1878.

And from Clifton College, too, stemmed an intellectual revival that led to an interest in higher education and the foundation of Bristol University College; the same fervour brought further education for women – something that was later to turn respectable Clifton ladies into suffragettes.

Clifton College was formally opened with a service in Big School on September 30th, 1862 with 60 boys, who listened to a sermon from the 25-year-old (and second choice) headmaster, the Rev. John Percival. Clifton, he said, would be "a place where all that is base or unworthy is hated and despised, a place where truth and uprightness and purity and all Christian virtue are held in honour."

The school, like Rugby, was divided into classical and modern sides and there was great enthusiasm for games. A junior school in Rodney Place was taken over. The ethos was muscular Christianity, with sermons about vileness and impure thoughts, The Feeble Character, and Manliness. One went: "Boys, it's your duty to be pure in heart. If you are not pure in heart, I'll flog you." Boys had to cover their knees when playing football and there were Sunday night "Jaws" on topics such as The Church of Rome and What Is A Gentleman?

The school was an immediate success and numbers grew incredibly quickly; by 1880 there were 600 boys. It was all due to Percival, who earned instant respect and love. "It is of great importance to the life of the school that there should be as little as possible of a barrier between masters and boys, that relations with them should be not so much professional as those of friends," he said.

Percival wanted to produce Christian gentlemen, not games-mad snobs but he could not entirely eradicate the snobbery: there was a prejudice against Town House day boys, and against non-athletic scholars. One old boy said the drawback to Clifton would always be the day boys "who don't add to its prestige at games or studies, the rubbish which daily pours out of the semi-detached villas with comforters rounds its neck, three-cornered

57

46. & 47. John Percival, first
headmaster of Clifton College
and, below, the College today.

notes in its pocket and querulous mamas and papas who each want a master to themselves in the background."

Certainly the success of Clifton made less well-off parents anxious to send their offspring to socially acceptable private schools, and dozens of genteel establishments were set up in the 1870s and 1880s. In 1888, the tally of schools in Clifton was incredible: for girls there were boarding and day schools in Windsor Terrace, St. Vincent's Parade, Badminton House, Clifton Park, Elmdale Road, Southernhay, Duncan House, Clifton Road, Kensington Villas, Melrose Place, Royal Park, Berkeley Square, Upper Belgrave Road, Meridian Place, Oakfield Road, Worcester Avenue, Apsley Road, Great George Street, Worcester Terrace, Duchess Road, The Avenue, Aberdeen Terrace, Anglesea Place, St. Pauls Road, the Mall and Cornwallis Grove.

For boys there were establishments at Whiteladies Road, Dowry Parade, Arlington Villas, West Park, Whiteladies Road, and Durdham Down – this smaller number reflecting the trend of sending boys to board away from home; or to the already established Bristol schools.

There were state or "board" schools at Anglesea Place, Bellevue, Berkeley Place, Brandon Hill, Hotwells, and Christ Church – now the Clifton library.

The Clifton Suspension Bridge, so long awaited, also brought big changes to the suburb: it made Clifton into a tourist attraction for day trippers and many said the place went downhill from 1864 onwards, because it became accessible from the other side, and encouraged building in Leigh Woods.

"With the completion of the Suspension Bridge, the erection of Clifton College and Clifton Down Hotel and a rapid increase of opulent inhabitants, why is there a cessation of Subscription Balls in Clifton? Bath and Cheltenham are now more interesting in winter," complained one socialite.

The bridge was certainly a long time arriving. Vick's bequest was made in 1753; Brunel won the competition to design it in 1830; the foundation stone was laid in 1831, and it finally opened on December 9th, 1864.

In June 1831 the Bridge Committee cleared a site on the Clifton side and on June 21st held a breakfast at the Bath Hotel, after which they assembled round a pile of stones which had been dug out.

Brunel, who called the bridge "my first love, my darling" then entered the circle, picked up a stone from the heap and handed it to Lady Elton, who made a short speech. Then there was a deafening discharge of cannon from below and the National Artillery played. Colours were run up flagstaffs and there was a champagne toast to the bridge.

The next ceremony was the laying of the Leigh abutment foundation stone in 1836, with fanfares, burial of a time capsule, and a dinner at the hotel which had ordered special commemorative china.

The actual building of the bridge was an entertainment in itself. "The work seems to go on in perfect silence, for at the distance at which we stand it is impossible to catch the slightest sound either of voice or implement. The workers suspended in mid-air are to our view scarcely as large as spiders and like spiders, the busy hands and feet seem to crouch and cluster upon a web airy and light as the gossamer's. One wonders how the men can maintain their position on a structure of apparent threads and still more how they can retain their self-possession and working faculties while balanced at the height of some 300 feet above the water."

Brunel, who died before the bridge was finished, made the first crossing in a basket suspended from a one and half inch thick iron bar across the chasm – it stuck halfway and he had to climb out to unstick it – and so many intrepid people wanted to copy him that a charge of 5s. was made. A honeymoon couple from Failand got stuck in the middle for an hour, swinging from the bar, which also made a handy hanger for political effigies, which were hung there for people to stone. George Gibbs of the Bristol gunsmiths' firm, and a crack shot, was asked to shoot down a particularly offensive effigy of a parliamentary candidate.

For the opening ceremony, special stands were built and these were ticket only, but an estimated 140,000 to 150,000 non-ticket holders turned up, as contemporary illustrations show. Flags waved, banners flew, bells rang and there was a ceremonial arch garlanded with flowers. A long civic procession opened the proceedings, leading to the first newspaper report of a traffic jam.

"Band after band poured forth their joyous strains, salvoes of artillery were being discharged, and all nature seemed animated and vocal with rejoicing," reported the *Western Daily Press*.

After the opening, a banquet in morning dress was held at the Victoria Rooms, and in the evening

THE STREET ORGAN NUISANCE

The hurdy gurdy, the trumpet and the fife, to say nothing of the ordinary street cries, the newspaper horns and occasionally two rival brass bands are within hearing at the same time, from seven in the morning until ten at night. The effects of these shocking discordant noises upon those among us who are invalids are very distressing. Our nerves are excruciated, our medical treatment greatly neutralised, our recovery painfully protracted. There are those who will take care not again to subject themselves to this in Clifton.

'Yours, Distressed', *Clifton Chronicle* **1859**.

WHERE'S THE POLICE (1)?

There are an unusual number of beggars and pickpockets who are celebrating the new year in the streets of Clifton, a swarm of beggars by whom Clifton is now infested. It needs only a daily walk through the streets to be assaulted by a succession of suppliants for relief, young or old, whose impertinent importunity is at once disagreeable and disgraceful.

Clifton Chronicle **editorial 1853**.

WHERE'S THE POLICE (2)?

I am subjected each evening on the beautiful Clifton Downs by a horde of half-clad Italian organ boys who, possessed of monkeys, guinea-pigs etc, pertinaciously harass each person . . . of course the police are never in sight.

'A Clifton Lady', *Clifton Chronicle* **1864**.

THE OYSTER NUISANCE

Three or four vendors with stentorian lungs howling bawling and yelling their shellfish two or three hours every night. Clifton has ceased to be a fit residence for the nervous, the sickly or the studious.

Clifton Chronicle, **1863**.

'DISGUSTED OF CLIFTON' WRITES TO THE EDITOR

DUST! DUST! DUST!

"Sir, I came to Clifton last Saturday three weeks with my family, purposing to remain for a couple of months but have now made arrangements to leave by the up express on Friday, being literally driven away by the dust. We know of four families of visitors about to quit your (in other respects) delightful watering place for the same reason, from a cause that might easily be remedied – watering of roads."

Letter to *Clifton Chronicle*, **1852**.

DIRT! DIRT! DIRT!

"Sir, Permit a visitor to your charming place to suggest that in the matter of scavenging (refuse collection) you are rather behind the times. Some heaps of straw and tan which have been swept up in front of the place at which I am presently staying have been suffered to remain for a couple of days before they were removed. Then again, your dust carts arrive in this neighbourhood in the afternoon, instead of early in the morning and the men who have charge of them are certainly not members of the teetotal society."

A Visitor to Princes Buildings, 1865.

BUILDING MANIA AGAIN

The March of the Masons

Many living have made hay [he meant literally] long since in Clifton Park. The little farmhouse where they sold fresh butter, near Litfield Place, will soon be shut out of sight by a cordon of domestic palaces. It seems but as yesterday that the Victoria Rooms and another building were the only edifices in the direction of Berkeley Square. A boy was brought before magistrates for milking a cow in Tyndall's Park into a pair of new boots which he was taking home to his master.

Bristol Times **editorial 1855**.

there was an electric light display on the bridge from 8–10pm. It was pronounced disappointing, "at times brilliant, at others dim." (The very first display of electric lighting in Clifton was at the Victoria Rooms in 1863, at a Grand Ball and Supper).

A few privileged people had been allowed to drive across the bridge before the ceremony, among them David Livingstone the famous explorer, but only foot traffic was allowed over the bridge that opening day, December 9th, 1864.

After the civic procession and the big-wigs had made the first crossing, it was opened to the public. First across was 21 year-old Mary Griffiths of Hanham, and we know this by an astonishing historical bridging of time; she made a broadcast about it for the BBC in 1936, when she was 93.

She went with her uncle to the Clifton side. "I was determined to get as near and to see as much as I could," she told listeners. "So I pushed up to the front and got right up to the gate that had been erected across the entrance to the bridge. When the signal was given and the gate was opened, I suddenly decided to be the first across, so I began to run.

"I had not run very far when I heard my uncle shout 'Run, Mary, run' and I turned round and saw a young man some yards behind me, running as fast as he could. I could see he was trying to beat me across and I tucked up my long dress and ran for dear life – and I beat him by a few yards!"

The cost of the grand opening ceremony to the Suspension Bridge Trust was £597, and unbeknown, another newsworthy event took place that day.

48. The bridge as it might have been: William Burge's unsuccessful competition entry.

49. & 50. Brunel's bridge under construction.

THE ILLUSTRATED LONDON NEWS

No. 1292.—VOL. XLV.　　　　SATURDAY, DECEMBER 17, 1864.　　　　WITH A SUPPLEMENT, FIVEPENCE

UTILISATION OF SEWAGE.

MATTERS intrinsically mean and repulsive sometimes affect so largely the well-being of communities as to assume an aspect of dignity. What more insignificant than the locust? Yet locusts, when organised, as they occasionally are, into an infinitely multitudinous host, and ravaging, as they sometimes will, vast breadths of country, command the affrighted attention of mankind. What topic more uninviting than sewage? Yet, as our own experience shows, it may rise into one of national importance. Hygiène, in certain stages of a people's development, becomes the most urgent of the practical sciences. It is so at this moment in the United Kingdom.

The rapid aggregation of men into large masses consequent on the expansion of manufacturing industry, and, perhaps, the natural but mistaken modes in which law has intervened for the preservation of the public health, have combined to present for solution one of the most difficult and pressing problems of the age, and one which the physical and social

OPENING OF THE CLIFTON SUSPENSION BRIDGE.—SEE PAGE 600.

51. The bridge opening in 1864 made the front page of the *Illustrated London News*.

52. A contemporary lithograph by J. Fagan published in 1864, the year the bridge opened.

While the rest of the family and relations went to the bridge opening, Mrs Clara Ames, a German-born countess who had married a Bristol businessman, entertained her lover Jardine Robinson at her home in Caledonia Place, an event which was to lead to a 1868 divorce case that scandalised not just Clifton but the whole country, because THREE co-respondents were named.

The new bridge drew enormous crowds in the first year, and as Latimer observed, seemed to possess "an irresistible attraction to persons afflicted with suicidal derangement."

The first suicide from the bridge was in May 1866 by Mr George Wellington Green, 51, who lived at Portishead. He was a family man whose brothers were a city alderman and a shipowner.

"He presented himself at the toll house and appeared to be in thoughtful mood, and was observed to press his hand to his head as if suffering from some painful sensation there. Almost immediately afterwards he placed his hands upon the railings of the bridge, which are about four feet high, and jumped over. His body was observed to twirl over as it descended and then to fall with a heavy thud upon the mud of the Avon, where the tide had receded.

Notwithstanding the terrific height and the fall, about 280 feet, no bones were broken and with the exception of some bruises on the temple, the body was not at all disfigured."

This was the first of over two hundred suicides to date; until comparatively recently, suicide was a criminal offence, so anyone who survived was liable to be charged, though in practice the magistrates were usually sympathetic. Often people took their lives for quite trivial reasons. Suicide number ten was servant Lucy Emma Durant, aged 19, who had a row with her young man and left her employer a note saying "pay my debts out of my wages as you will not see me again."

Cotton worker Sarah Ann Henley was the first to jump and survive, in 1885, when her skirts acted like

53. Mary Griffiths, who as a young girl was the first member of the public to cross the bridge on the opening day.

"It seems to me that every person within sight of it finds the first thought a melancholy one, and the talk of every visitor is suicide."

Talk of suicides was bad for Clifton trade and by now the main shopping streets were well established, and considered by the rest of Bristol to be very expensive and exclusive.

Aspiring shop keepers wanted to open a branch in the suburb – despite Cliftonians' reputation for being slow payers of bills – and John Brooks the dry cleaner opened his in 1863, just a few doors away from the branch that is still trading. This is the only centenarian survivor in Clifton, for the rest of the businesses still trading have moved away or been absorbed into other concerns.

Drycleaning was badly needed, for Victorian clothes were rarely washable. The new process involved taking the garment to pieces, soaking it in naptha and then reassembling it, and only the wealthy could afford it – Brooks at 11 Victoria Street advertised in 1865 that the firm was patronised by the Duke of Beaufort.

a parachute and saved her. The resident bridge inspector Thomas Stevens saw her turn a complete somersault and float over the riverbank, carried by the wind. Workmen near the Cumberland Basin could not believe their eyes and were reluctant to give help. When two bystanders finally dragged her out, a passing cab driver demanded £10 guarantee against damage to his vehicle to take the mud-plastered girl to the Bristol Royal Infirmary. Sarah lived to the age of 84 and died in 1948.

As the number of deaths increased, Cliftonians began to make suggestions to prevent jumps from the bridge; one was for a complicated system of coiled nets held by springs which when touched would unfurl into a hammock and catch the leaper, at the same time ringing an alarm bell in the toll lodge.

Those anxious to promote Clifton as a tourist resort felt the suicides gave the place a bad image.

54. Photographer Fred Bromhead set up his first studio at Number 1 Regent Street, Clifton in the 1880s.

55. T.C. Marsh: the men's department in 1922.

"J. Brooks, Dyer, tends his grateful acknowledgements to the Nobility, Clergy and Gentry for the liberal support with which they have honoured him and begs to inform them that he has removed to Nelson Place, Clifton (opposite his former establishment) where he hopes for a continuance of their patronage."

Bromheads, now in Whiteladies Road, opened their Clifton Photographic Company at 1 Regent Street in the late 1870s; Thomas Culverwell Marsh's shop opened in the same street in 1877, and later advertised as "hosier, hatter, shirtmaker, Indian and Colonial outfitter, at the corner of Boyce's Avenue and Clifton Down."

Garaways, the eighteenth century nurserymen, were still trading on an ever-shrinking patch of land west of Whiteladies Road, and the St. Vincent's Rocks Hotel was set up in 1868 by a newly formed joint stock company to exploit the popularity of the new Suspension Bridge, in a house that had been a boarding house almost continuously since it was built in the 1780s.

There seems to have been a chemist's shop on the corner of The Mall, ever since the street was set out: a major occupier was John Mortimer, inventor of Mortimer's Odontalgine, a remedy for toothache, and Mortimer's Pectin Balsam for colds, coughs and asthma. The building until recently housing Lloyds Bank in Regent Street had been a bank since 1862.

Other survivors are Alexandra Workwear, which in its Victorian heyday was The Alexandra, a large linen drapery firm with a department store in Whiteladies Road and W.H. Smith, whose first shop, as opposed to railway stall, opened at 24 Regent Street. They also had a lending library at Whiteladies Gate.

But closed down quite recently are Steer and Geary who, like T.C. Marsh, made a living from selling local school uniforms, and Lennards, whose imposing headquarters, known as Lennard's Corner, was demolished by the bomb on the Triangle in 1940.

One great Clifton institution long since vanished was Cordeux's – everyone called it "Cordews". This family of drapers traded first in St. James Barton

The Alexandra Co.,

WEST PARK CORNER and
WHITE LADIES' ROAD . . | CLIFTON.

THE

Great Winter Sale

WILL COMMENCE ON

MONDAY NEXT, Jan. 2nd
1905.

Most Attractive
Bargains
WILL BE FOUND IN EVERY DEPARTMENT.

POST & TELEPHONE ORDERS
receive immediate attention.
TELEPHONE No. 1344.

We Close on Saturdays at 2 o'clock,
Other Evenings, including Wednesdays, at 7 o'clock.

56. & 57. The Alexandra
shop in Whiteladies Road.

MR DICKENS AT THE VICTORIA ROOMS

There was a tolerably numerous attendance on Wednesday and on Friday the large room was crowded in every part. It is superfluous to say that a great intellectual treat was afforded and that Mr Dickens now moved his hearers to laughter and anon melted them to tears as he graphically delineated the creations of his genius.

Clifton Chronicle, **May 1866.**

THE QUEEN'S HOTEL [now Habitat] OPENS

It is the most complete and perfect of its kind in the kingdom. The various apartments for the accommodation of visitors have been furnished with exquisite taste; the bedrooms are model dormitories; and the whole arrangements of the hotel such as leave nothing to be desired.

Clifton Chronicle, **October 1854.**

CLIFTON SNOBBERY

It is not an uncommon thing to hear residents who draw from the trade of Bristol the money on which they depend . . . talking, in the true spirit of "snob", of Clifton having become quite vulgar since the 'tagrag' of Bristol have taken so much resort to it.

1860s political pamphlet.

DEATH OF A SERVANT GIRL

Mary Ann Rogers (17) met a dreadful and untimely death under deplorable circumstances. She had been in service nine weeks at 5 Tottenham Place, when in the kitchen at 4pm her clothing caught fire when a poker fell out of the coals onto her while she was stoning the hearth, and set her alight.

Clifton Chronicle, **1861.**

A CLIFTON SCHOOLBOY'S DIARY, 1879–1885

Aged 13. Bought walking sticks and went for walks, played tennis, fives, ball games, vingt et un, arranged albums, had private theatricals, made drawings, played chess and whist, lounged, lay in hammocks, projected a fishing expedition, fought sham duels with pistols, bought arrows and fired them on the Downs from ancient bows to the imminent danger of the public till turned off by the Ranger, threw the cricket ball.

Aged 18. The craze for bicycles was rising to its height and Henry bought a Tangent with a 52 in. front wheel and solid rubber tyres, while I had to be content with a bone-shaker. It was made of oak with iron tyres and for a long time defied my utmost efforts to tame it. It was a very ugly thing to fall off or with or under or all three, I eventually learned to ride by inventing a method now in vogue for teaching servant girls at dusk. The hire was 5s. 6d and it was virtually indestructible.

Aged 19. I did chemical experiments, ate ices at Pomeroys, visited all the swimming baths, bought flies for fishing, played croquet and tennis, went by steam to Cumberland basin from Hotwells, visited City Museum, and played cricket everywhere and with everybody, including girls. Went for bicycle rides, played fives and card games, went to the Zoo, the dentist, did holiday task, got a Jeffries racquet at Drylands [This was a sports shop on the end of Caldonia Place, where the bank is: Dryland was Clifton's professional cricket coach]. Went to Bristol.

Francis Newbolt's *A Diary Of A Fag.*

FOOD AT CLIFTON COLLEGE, 1870s.

Breakfast: tea or coffee with bread and butter and cold meat.
Dinner: meat and pudding or on two days of the week soup and meat, with beer.
Tea: tea with bread and butter.
Supper: bread and cheese or butter with beer or milk.

and Castle Street but two of the Cordeux sons, Charles and John ventured into the wealthy suburb of Clifton.

Charles the watchmaker and jeweller started trading in the Quadrant in 1859 and John opened his Linen and Longcloth Warehouse at 6 Carlton Place (where Focus is now) in the following year. His empire grew; he opened another shop in Regent Street next to the old Post Office in 1869, and his brother moved in next door at Carlton Place.

In 1880 he advertised that "the John Cordeux and Sons business which was commenced scarcely 20 years ago with only about seven yards of counter in a very small shop has grown day by day in Public Favour until now Ladies can ask for almost anything with the certainty of having the want supplied."

Cordeux bought up shops and properties adjoining and opened more and more showrooms to sell things like the new Mlle Bernhardt cap in silk and satin trimmed with cream Spanish lace, 2s.6d. – 3s.11d. He gradually acquired all the property on the corner of Merchants Road and most of Regent Street, from where Hartwells garage is now down to Saville Place, apart from the Post Office and a few shops like Prossers, and the bank, which would not sell up.

The result was a department store that sold everything, furnishings, clocks, carpets, toys, as well as linens and fashions, in great profusion, very cheaply. Clifton shoppers were very ambivalent about Cordeux's: it was extremely convenient, they delivered, they made up fashions, but they were slightly vulgar and not at all exclusive. They advertised on the side of the horse buses and piled underwear high in their window displays.

The store was designed as a thoroughfare so that you could walk from Merchants Road to Regent Street through the shop. Inside, should you suddenly receive an overseas posting, you could buy Indian Colonial and Wedding outfits at short notice, and goods could be forwarded to all parts of the world – they even sold special regulation cases for the Indian Parcel Post.

"A lordly treasure house" was how one commentator described it in the 1890s. "A tour of inspection through the numerous departments is like a visit to one of the most gorgeous bazaars of the Orient. Agencies in every part of the globe contribute to the lavish display."

The store employed 300 assistants in 45 departments spread over 25,000 sq. feet and supplied schools, colleges and hotels and institutions with linens. The shop front had 43 windows and upstairs there was room for 400 hands to work at making up and alterations. The main showroom for Ladies' Fashions was 70 feet long.

But John Cordeux junior obviously over-reached himself. Mrs. Trapnell in her memoir of Clifton remembered him standing outside the entrance muttering "O Lord, send them in, send them in". In January 1909, he announced the shop was closing for alterations, extensions, redecoration and a refit, but this was a fiction – it was the last gasp. In May 1911 the shop was closed down, with assets of £60,081 and a deficit of £49,998. He had a big overdraft and mortgage, and had to sell up to satisfy his creditors.

But enough assets and stock remained to open on a more modest scale in Queen's Road, at 48, 50 and 52, Royal Promenade, in 1913.

Perversely, having failed to support him in Clifton, shoppers now complained when he moved. "By the closing of Messrs Cordeux's premises many Clifton householders who have been in the habit of shopping there will be put to considerable inconvenience," thundered one aggrieved customer.

The new Cordeux shop was sold in 1928 to Bobby's who made it the basis for their big new Bristol branch: they became Brights, and this in turn became Dingles, so a little echo of the Cordeux tradition still remains in Clifton. In the meantime his empty Clifton empire was taken over by Ernest Crichton and his Piano Emporium.

58. The influential Sturge family epitomised the growing emancipation of Victorian women.

"The most dreary place in the world"

A terrible respectability fell on Clifton as it celebrated its golden jubilee as a suburb, and with it came bigotry about class and religion.

Parallel to the social divisions were the religious ones. Clifton Parish Church and Christchurch were low church, but by the 1860s there was move towards high church Anglicanism, thanks to the Oxford Movement, which led to the building of All Saints' in Pembroke Road in 1872, with 800 seats. Add to this a fair-sized Catholic population and a terror of Popery, and the ingredients for a religious war are in place. What's more, leading members of the Oxford Movement came to live in Clifton, and wrote seditious pamphlets.

(Clifton had a long history of resistance to any high church tendencies: when the leader of the Oxford Movement, Edward Pusey, whose daughters Lucy and Mary were at school in Royal York Crescent, proposed to preach at Clifton Parish Church in 1845, the church elders threatened that they would walk out "with marked and significant stamping movements" if he mounted the pulpit)

Francis Newman, brother of the notorious Cardinal who 'went over' to Rome lived in Clifton, but he disapproved of his brother's conversion and preferred vegetarianism. He used to carry lentil sandwiches in his pockets and lived until he was 90, which must prove something.

From a modern point of view it is hard to imagine obscure theological points causing pages of debate in the local newspapers, but at the time everyone went to church or chapel: attendances were enormous, for it never occurred to anyone not to attend. So the life of the church and its particular theology were immensely important.

The letters in the *Clifton Chronicle*, which was upmarket, conservative and therefore low church, reveal a hideous intolerance of the high church adherents, and as for theological rows, the one to top it all was an 1874 battle that became nationally famous: Jenkins v Cook.

The Rev. Flavel Cook was the vicar of Christchurch and Henry Jenkins of Vyvyan Terrace was a member of the congregation who wrote a theological book which inspired the Vicar's disapproval. So Cook refused him Communion and the ensuing row ended with a hearing before the Church Commissioners, the first of its kind since the Reformation.

The hearing went on for weeks and had Clifton agog. When the verdict came, the *Chronicle* actually had a queue of paperboys waiting for the 1,000 extra copies it had printed. And the verdict ruined Cook who had to resign his living and pay the heavy costs of the case.

The religious rows were invariably petty – when the Pro-cathedral in Park Place was built in 1850 there were cries about "No Popery" over the statues designed for the porch, and lectures would be delivered at the Victoria Rooms on "Papal aggression". Real Clifton, west of Pembroke Road, was equally snooty about non-conformism, which was confined to poor Hotwells and the unfashionable east side of Whiteladies Road, jokingly known as the Via Sacra because of all its churches.

The rivalry between low and high church led to a kind of religious guerilla warfare: parishioners of Christchurch wrote to the Bishop with complaints of ritualist acts at All Saints. They complained that they "used candles for show not lighting, that clergy turned their back on the congregation during Communion, that they wore a vestment known as a manciple and made the sign of the cross and bowed." All this was "the foolery of Rome."

This absorption in religion meant that vicars had great influence and often behaved autocratically. Mourant Brock, vicar of Christchurch 1855–1872, for example, caused turmoil by summarily dismissing "without notice or excuse the whole of the male teachers at Christchurch Sunday school, as he thought by having female teachers he would have them more entirely under his authority."

"This arbitrary conduct estranged him from many who had been his warm supporters and formed one of the many mistakes he made, resulting from a swelled head. He was very dramatic and sensational in the pulpit – he called wealth "yellow clay" – and he often astonished the congregation by his plain speaking. In manner he was arrogant and

59. & 60. No Popery in Clifton! The Pro-Cathedral in Park Place and the High Church All Saints' in Pembroke Road enraged many Clifton residents.

dictatorial and he had a great sense of his own importance," says Freeman in his *Worthies.*

While the wealthy Clifton flourished in righteousness in the 1860s and 1870s, thanks to another building boom, Hotwells as usual was suffering. It had become a notoriously poor district to live in because of a slump in the port and shipping.

An 1867 letter headed 'Great Destitution in Hotwells' said: "Great numbers of poor shivering, starving creatures during this inclement weather have been relieved by meals of bread and cheese at the Mendicity Office. About 20 cases of very great destitution in the Hotwells are being investigated at present." Cholera broke out there the following summer.

The Clifton Mendicity Association was an organisation which helped beggars. The Clifton Loan Blanket Scheme lent out 230 blankets in 1861 and in six winters had lost only three, showing the appreciation of its benefit by the poor of the parish.

"Because of stagnation in their trade, of 350 shipwrights, 300 were out of employment," reported a Clifton curate. "They do not like to ask for relief and consequently are nearly starving. They have pledged everything valuable, watches, wedding rings, etc. Labourers, sawyers, plasterers, masons, painters and small shopkeepers are out of work: a quarter of the working class is unemployed."

Clifton ladies played an important part in alleviating local poverty, for good works were about the only real work that social convention allowed them.

They ran the Blanket Society and Temperance League, they became District Visitors, a kind of amateur social worker who told the poor how to clean their homes and cook and budget – rich, one might say, when they themselves had servants – and they propped up the church mission, the Sunday school, and the church bazaar. They went to sewing parties to make shirts and baby clothes for the poor, and they doled out the free sick notes for Clifton Dispensary to the sick women who trudged from tradesman's entrance to basement begging for one.

And these worthy women had daughters. When their sons began to benefit from the education they were able to obtain at Clifton College, parents began to want something better than the foolish and frivolous "academies" for their daughters. Percival at Clifton was all in favour of better education for girls and higher education for women, and made the idea acceptable.

So in 1868 the Clifton Association for Promoting Higher Education of Women was formed. Clifton ladies began to agitate in a genteel way for the vote, and a local suffrage society was started. By 1874 it was part of the National Society for Women's Suffrage and run from 53 Park Street, and the members were almost exclusively middle class.

In Clifton it was obvious what was at stake. In 1869 an Act of Parliament conferred municipal franchise on women, so the names of 641 female ratepayers in Clifton appeared on the electoral roll. The new voters ensured that three Clifton Liberals lost their seats.

Women's suffrage was naturally frowned on by respectable Clifton and so was any idea that servants might have rights and join a union. This sarcastic parody letter appeared in the *Chronicle* in 1874, purporting to be from Sarah Ann, Clifton servant.

"Ai were reading your paper on Wensday as i always do afore i takes it up to master, and i sees among the news something about forming a national trades union of working women. So i says to Mary Jane as how our time had come and that the missesses should no longer have it just how they pleased. i think we as cooks the meat might as well have the first cut at it. i sees no reason why we as belong to the union should not in time sit in the drawing room." All the same, the Bristol Branch of the Union of Working Women was operating from Park Street by 1879.

But Clifton women were beginning to have an intellectual and social influence. The Winkworth sisters who lived at 31 Cornwallis Crescent, and from 1874 at 21 Victoria Square, were typical.

In 1872, Susannah, the practical one, was a district visitor managing a Sanitary Mission to show the poor how to disinfect their homes and keep them clean, and this experience made her realise how difficult it was for the "decent poor" to find apartments in respectable houses.

In Hotwells she wished to provide accommodation for a few such families and thought that if some of the big Georgian houses were bought and improved, the character of the whole neighbourhood would improve too.

So she spent a considerable sum (which she never got back in rent) on doing up two houses in Dowry Square and two in Chapel Row "at that time inhabited by a very rough and low set of people" and finding respectable tenants for them. The cellars were turned into wash-houses and coal stores

61. Clifton High School cricket team in 1892. W.G. Grace's daughter, Bessie, stands second from the left.

"to obviate the necessity of keeping coals in cupboards in the room."

Her idea of model appartments, with a superintendent (a role she played at first) to see that the rent was paid and order was kept, worked very well and "the whole tone of the Square was raised," and this led her to organise in 1874 the building of a large Scots baronial appartment block for the decent poor, in Jacob's Wells Road. Each flat had a balcony and water and a gas supply, and proof that the scheme worked came with the low figures for infection and disease.

Her bluestocking sister Catherine, friend of Charlotte Bronte, Mrs Gaskell and other major literary figures, was more concerned with education for women and was involved in the creation of Clifton High School, and in setting up higher education lectures for women. In 1871 she reported; "We have 200 students, all girls who have left school and they really work so well and write such clever papers and I am quite amazed at them sometimes."

Clifton High School opened in January 1878, at 65 Pembroke Road: the money had been raised by selling £20 shares, each one of which entitled the holder to a nomination place.

Plans were hatched at 12 meetings held at John Percival's house in 1877: the idea was "to supply to girls on moderate terms general instruction of the highest class." One of the first pupils, Ellen Openshaw remembered her father telling her: "At last education is beginning for girls; a school is to be started where they are taught from the blackboard and from the heart and soul of the teacher."

The first head was Mary Alice Woods, who set out three principles: religious freedom, no class distinction and no competition. The latter did not last very long. The school was an instant success despite misgivings from some sections of society – high schools at that time were considered dangerous because girls of different class could mix, and it was thought that they would be in moral danger from having to travel on public transport.

(The hockey-playing high school girl was also thought rather fast and tomboyish, until made respectable by Angela Brazil. The Duchess of Northumberland said she would rather see her daughters stand at a washtub than be pupils at a high school)

74

62. & 63. A run-down Blackboy Hill in 1885 and a more salubrious stretch of Whiteladies Road.

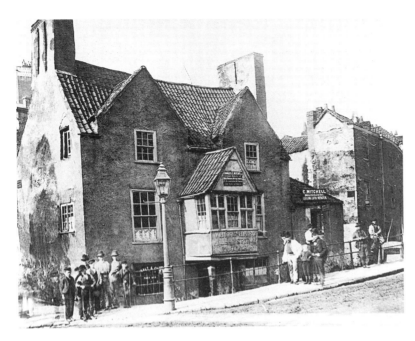

64. The old face of Jacobs Wells: the White Hart Inn at the bottom of the hill in 1877.

65. Susannah Winkworth's 'model industrial dwellings' made way in the 1950s for a modern block of flats.

An early teacher wrote: "Readers acquainted with Clifton will readily understand the sort of criticism we encountered, criticism from parents who objected to what they called the 'mixture', i.e. of classes, from heads of private schools who thought their interests endangered or perhaps from a doting mother who demanded concessions to the educational style, which was certainly influenced by Clifton College."

Within a year the numbers were up to 160 and in 1879 the school moved out to houses in Worcester Avenue, which was gradually bought up and closed off, as now. Percival made his daughter Bessie a foundation pupil and W.G. Grace sent his daughter there and would watch her playing cricket with a soft ball and skirts down to the ankle. The five Sturge daughters were all educated there; the Newbolts also enrolled their daughter.

The movement to educate women gained momentum when University College opened in 1876, because women were admitted right from the beginning. Bristol University College's extension courses were an integral part of the philosophy and non-academic girls and women could attend lectures given by university staff.

Women at University were of course a great novelty. Marion Pease described the first day at University College, then a house at 32 Park Row. She walked across Durdham Down with her friend and fellow student Amy Bell (who became the first woman stockbroker) and caught a tram to the top of Park Street.

Women students were given a small cloakroom. "It was furnished with three or four wooden chairs and a small deal table and with pegs for our heavy cloth waterproofs. Here we worked and ate our lunch we had brought with us and here in spite of the surroundings I think I spent some of the happiest hours of my life – with new friends and those talks which at 18 seemed so exciting."

The five daughters of the famous surveying family, the Sturges, all benefitted from a better education: Emily at 33 was the first woman on the Bristol School Board, and supported the suffragettes, Elizabeth interested herself in housing reform and in the Red Lodge reformatory, Mary obtained her MA, Helen did missionary work and stood for Bristol City Council and Caroline eventually qualified as a doctor in the 1890s.

For women who did not qualify for the university there had been since 1868 the lectures for ladies, on a wide assortment of subjects, biology, astronomy, botany, George III, the Renaissance, painting, and so on. Elizabeth Sturge revealed what a treat it was for Clifton:

"We read delightedly and every week handed in papers signed by a number or a pseudonym – such was the dread at that time of having your name known in such a connection. There was great excitement when the lists were read out – some who had not attained to the position they hoped for were even known to weep!

"There were large numbers of young women who could never have hoped to become students at Oxford or Cambridge and for their benefit a system of local lectures to ladies was established. We were fortunate in having in Clifton a circle of enlightened men and women by whom the idea was warmly taken up . . . of course such a method of study was very unsystematic, one jumped from one subject to another but the mental stimulus was of lasting value."

Education of women inevitably led to an increased awareness of the lack of women's rights, and the first moves towards women's suffrage in Bristol had most of their roots in respectable Clifton and Redland – for it was at first a very middle class movement that only gradually extended to include the working class girls in the factories and shops.

The ladies who began to agitate were taking some social risk; they were wives or daughters of prominent men, like Mrs Dove Willcox, wife of a JP, Mary Estlin, daughter of the famous Bristol preacher, Mrs Beddoe, wife of the doctor, Florence Hill, daughter of Commissioner Hill.

They could have made their feelings public only with male consent and indeed a circular about the first meeting, at 3, The Mall on January 24th, 1868 explained that it was being held there with the permission of the Commissioner.

Mrs Beddoe, describing that first meeting said: "I found a large party of the fashionable part of the community present." When it transpired that a petition was to be signed calling for votes for women "in a few minutes the audience disappeared as quickly as a flight of birds."

But the movement was unstoppable, and caused a local backlash, for in the late 1870s a Clifton branch of the Anti-Suffrage League was formed.

By 1883 the Clifton suffragists were holding open meetings on the Downs; the *Bristol Mercury* reports 12 successive evening meetings, at which Maria

SWINDLERS AND SHOPLIFTERS IN CLIFTON

Brigit and Jane Brook, apparently young, though they gave their ages as 50 and 60, were charged with begging in West Mall. When searched they had £6 on their persons, and were begging on pretence that they were asking for relief for orphans so that they could emigrate to Australia. Sentenced to one month's hard labour.

Clifton Chronicle 1863

Three respectably dressed women were charged with stealing six woollen shawls worth £5. 19s. 6d. from Mr Wyatt, draper of 4 and 5 Mall. They had made small purchases and distracted him.

Clifton Chronicle, 1863.

A SMALL TRAGEDY

On Saturday morning the body of an infant was discovered, wrapped in an old newspaper, lying in the path from the Observatory to Clifton Down.

Clifton Chronicle, 1856.

THIS SPORTING LIFE

Clifton Rugby Club, founded 1872. The game to be played as at Clifton College but Rule 19 to say 'no kicking or tripping to be allowed'. The colours to be black and lavender, 20 players a side. The match to be decided by the majority of goals, no matter how many tries a side scored. Rule 11: 'No hacking with the heel ABOVE the knee is fair'.

Rules of Clifton Bicycle Club, founded 1878. "A horse shall never be passed on both sides at once." "The Club will pay the expenses of any member who prosecutes a person for stone or cap throwing or other mischievous interference with bicyclists."

Captain Niblett, president.

[The Clifton Football Club, founded in 1882, came to a parting of the ways with other Bristol teams in 1896–7, after playing Kingswood, when the crowd rioted over a Clifton player who kicked an opponent. Clifton team was pronounced too rough and too snooty and was dropped from the fixture lists. There were also complaints that W.G. Grace, captain of Gloucestershire cricket team, tended to pick all his players from the public schools and the university, instead of using Bristol boys.]

SERVANT LIFE

The Domestic Servants' Institution in Dover Place, Clifton furnishes at moderate charges lodgings for female servants of good character, who must bring with them a satisfactory reference.

Advertisement, 1875.

Rules for removing Boys or Girls from the workhouse as servants. They must be paid not less than 1s a week, plus clothing, and to be employed at a trade not more than 10 and half hours a day, exclusive of meals. *Clothing for boys*: 2 jackets, 2 waistcoats, 2 trousers, braces, 2 caps, 2 shirts, 2 prs stockings, 2 handkerchiefs, 2 neckerchiefs, 2 prs boots, 1 small toothcomb, 1 brush, 1 comb, 1 clothes box, 1 Bible, 1 prayer book. *Girls*: 2 frocks, 2 skirts, 2 flannel petticoats, 1 pr stays, 2 handkerchiefs, 2 night caps, 2 prs stockings, 2 bonnets, 1 shawl, 1 cape and then as boys.

Clifton Poor Law Union, 1874.

SCANDAL, 1871

The prevailing gossip in Clifton during the past few days has related to a fracas which took place outside the Clifton Club. It would seem that a middle aged gentleman had been paying his addresses to a certain young lady by whom he had become enamoured.

The proposed alliance did not meet with approval from her relatives and her two brothers waylaid the captain and thrashed him with sticks. The captain did his best to defend himself but during the struggle his head was cut open and was bleeding profusely when the police arrived.

ANIMAL CRUELTY

The Zoo. I write these few lines on behalf of the poor lion in the Zoological Gardens. For some weeks past he has been slowly but surely dying, it is SHEER CRUELTY to leave him to die by inches. To those who saw this noble beast six months ago he now presents a pitiable appearance. Within little more than six months there have died a young leopard, a young lion, two lioness. Nearly all the monkeys are dead. A very fine pair of leopards has been sold leaving indeed a second pair, but the female is a poor specimen and the male hobbles about on three legs.

"Humanitas", Clifton Chronicle, **1871.**

IT REALLY IS APPALLING . . .

The state of Hotwells. I have many a time heaved a heavy sigh over the changing scenes in the Hotwells, compared with thirty years ago. The Hotwell House is boarded up, a receptacle for all sorts of rubbish. There were two splendid hotels, the Cumberland and the Hibernian, and a nice rank of lodging houses all of which have been swept away for dock improvement. Void ground is now used for boys to play pitch and toss and smaller children to make mudpies. Why not let the ground for building sites? Here is a chance for putting up houses of medium size and rent. Surely someone will look down on the now so utterly forsaken and neglected place.

Clifton Chronicle, **1878.**

Sir, I must Protest at the wanton destruction of trees in the enclosure adjoining Boyce's Avenue. It was previously one of the most charming parts of Clifton before the ruthless felling: And what for? To build shops. We do not need more shops.

Clifton Chronicle, **1878.**

The land at the top of the Zig Zag is a disgrace. Posts projecting from the ground are liable to upset the unwary pedestrian or nervous invalid. There are no proper seats, just narrow wooden slabs rotting with age.

Clifton Chronicle, **1879.**

HOUSE TO LET, 1871

To be let on Clifton Down, a well built first class MANSION (with separate wall and space between it and the adjoining house) comprising on ground floor, well ventilated hall with fireplace, 2 drawing rooms, dining room, library, butler's pantry and water closet. On the 1st floor, 4 bedrooms, dressing room and water closet, half space rooms for a cloakroom and bathroom. On basement floor, billiard room, servants' hall, large kitchen, back kitchen, wine cellar, coal cellar, dairy, water closet etc. Stabling with 2 stalls and 2 looseboxes, coach house, cottage for coachman, cottage for groom or gardener. [This was Birchfield, now renamed, near the Mansion House.]

A WORD OF ADVICE

Victoria Swimming Baths opens to Ladies. A word of advice on the subject of dress. If the heavy flannel dress usual in the sea is adopted, which impedes all freedom of motion in the water, without the breezes and open spaces of the sea beach, can scarcely be dried, and if this is used, the bath for ladies can never become popular. Let the dress consist of drawers reaching from the waist to the knees and of a tight fitting Garibaldi jacket or vest fastened at the waist and without sleeves, close round the neck to adapt it better for forward movement. It may have a short skirt but not full. Let these be of very lightest flannel or serge so as to retain as little water as possible.

Clifton Chronicle, **1871.** [**The pool opened, for men only, in 1850**]

DRUNK AT A FUNERAL

I have never seen in any town in England or on the Continent so much drunkeness as on Saturday night at the Hotwells and in Bristol but on Friday night as I was walking through the Triangle, I was obliged to witness one of the men who was driving a mourning coach so beastly drunk that before descending Park Street the mourners all left the coach whilst the drunken man was dragged from the box.

CLIFTON CHARACTERS

Frederick Hiles, aka Bartram, was a poor Hotwells lad who at the age of eight was horribly injured in a tram accident in 1880, when he lost both arms at the shoulder. But he was determined to be an artist and learned to hold the brush in his mouth. He changed his name and at 16 exhibited at the Bristol Academy of Fine Arts and later studied in Paris.

He designed postcards for Raphael Tuck, and came back with his wife and children to Bristol in 1906 to live in a small house on Constitution Hill. He was a familiar figure in his Inverness cape, and became a member of the Bristol Savages, and an R.A. in 1908; the City Art Gallery once had two of his pictures. By the 1920s he had developed severe gangrene and he fell into a depression and died in 1927.

Emma Marshall (1830–1899), prolific fictionaliser of Bristol's history, lived at 2 Victoria Square and later Worcester Terrace, had nine children and in 1878 her husband James's bank failed and he left his family with great debts. Emma wrote to keep the family, and took in boarders for Clifton High School. She wrote nearly 200 pieces, including 40 novels, the most famous being *In Colston's Days* and *Bristol Diamonds*.

Dr. John Addington Symonds of Clifton Hill House (and father of the poet) was the most popular doctor in Clifton. "He seemed to be the daily companion of each of us, so certain were we when we stepped out of our house or even looked out of our windows, to see Dr. Symonds and his carriage," said his 1871 obituary. He came to Bristol in 1831 "a tall refined good looking man with classical features, dark hair and whiskers, very gentle and suave in manner, invariably dressed in well-fitting black clothes and probably enjoyed the best and most extensive practice in the West of England. His well-horsed brougham, always proceeding at a tearing pace, was a well known object in Clifton."

Dr. Eliza Walker-Dunbar, Bristol's first woman doctor, lived in Oakfield Road and in the 1880s was a suffragette and feminist. In 1873 she was appointed house surgeon at the Children's Hospital but she was "compelled to relinquish the post in consequence of the hostile reaction of the rest of the medical staff, who resigned in a body," says Latimer.

General Worrall, of the landowning family, tall and grim, worked for the East India company, and had a blustering manner and loud voice. He was in his element at the Clifton Club in the Mall where in the 1880s he would hold forth about the iniquities of the government and the War Office, to prove that "the Army, Sir, is going to the dogs."

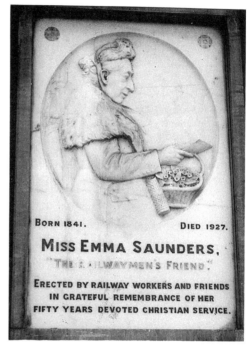

BORN 1841.   DIED 1927.
MISS EMMA SAUNDERS,
"THE RAILWAYMEN'S FRIEND."
ERECTED BY RAILWAY WORKERS AND FRIENDS
IN GRATEFUL REMEMBRANCE OF HER
FIFTY YEARS DEVOTED CHRISTIAN SERVICE.

66.

Emma Saunders (1841–1927), the Railwaymen's Friend who has a plaque outside Temple Meads station lived at Sion Hill. In her garden she grew flowers which she made up into buttonholes to cheer up the railway workers. She gave each railway carter a copy of *Black Beauty* to improve their treatment of their horses, provided refreshment and recreation rooms, and looked after railway families. She would even pay for their false teeth, and always provided an annual tea.

When she died her little coffin was carried on the shoulders of four high ranking uniformed men, along the street from her home to Christchurch, followed by a throng of railwaymen of all grades in their working uniform, each with a daffodil button-hole.

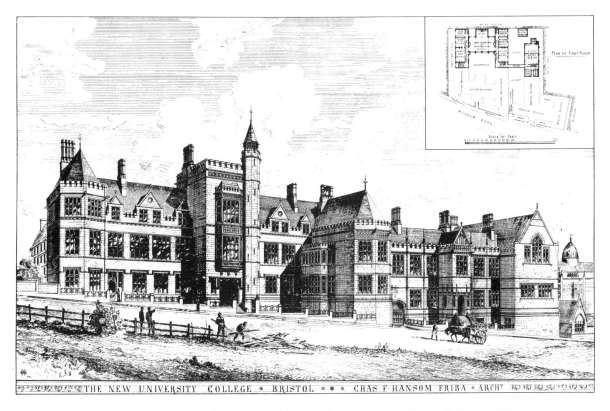

67. University College buildings proposed by Charles Hansom, architect of Clifton College.

Colby, the organiser, told the public: "Objections to our claims are based on the idea that the primary duty of woman is to darn stockings."

Female solidarity grew: In 1889 the striking cotton workers of Barton Hill marched to Clifton where the employers and directors lived, as did the sweet girls in 1892.

The big decision for the middle class suffragists was whether to take direct action or not and this issue split them apart. Half continued to campaign through debate and discussion but the rest went in for more violent means of persuasion, as will be seen later on.

While Clifton women were on the whole having a more interesting life, thanks to further education, and more freedom for fun – a gang of 22 Clifton ladies stormed the Clifton Cricket Club in 1890 and started up their own game – the rest of Clifton went on in its stolid, decent way and the suburb began to get a reputation for being appallingly dull, as well as snobbish.

A Dr. Graham Everett wrote an article, "Clifton as seen by an outsider, 1888," which offended everyone greatly.

"Local jealousies, an utter absence of a spirit of co-operation and enterprise among the inhabitants repel and drive away strangers. Unlike Bath, even in the days of its prosperity, Clifton was as dull as ditchwater, very nearly as dull as its modern representation, if dullness of so impenetrable a character can ever hope to be equalled with beauties of situation and scenery which render it naturally attractive," he claimed.

"Clifton, owing to the exclusiveness of its parvenu aristocracy, ridiculed by Sheridan in *School for Scandal*, combined with the absence of any sort of amusement, is the last place which any fashionable doctor would be mad enough to consign a consumptive patient."

This exchange was reported in the *Chronicle*:
Lady on holiday: "Do you know Clifton? I am going to Clifton for a time while my son is at Clifton College."
Another lady: "I pity you. I was there for three

miserable years. It is the most dreary place in the world; pretty enough but one can't always be admiring scenery and there is really nothing to do there and nothing to see."

Some Cliftonians agreed with the criticism: "Clifton is not improving as it should and the shops are not all attractive in appearance. Boyce's Avenue is like a back street, the shops are mean in appearance and seem not to have proper dwelling rooms attached to them and the road is filthy with refuse from the various provisions shops.

"Then again the Mall looks very ancient. One certainly does not expect to see in the main street of a fashionable place like Clifton two or three uncooked joints hung outside over a doorway and heavy looking cold pudding in the window. This is certainly more suited to a back street. It gives a bad appearance to the place and makes it decidedly common as does hanging materials outside a draper's shop to be fingered by every nurse-girl."

Something had to be done.

SEX AT CLIFTON COLLEGE, 1880s

When a boy was seen kissing a girl he was sent for the next day and presented with a religious book. 'This is a purely scientific matter,' observed the housemaster. 'Falling in love is like wine – it may be a good article of diet but not for boys at school.' Sentimental friendships which at times were mildly epidemic and usually arose from the dearth of female companionship, were condemned as 'bad form'. However this maybe, these idealisations of younger by older boys were a matter of great unease and perplexity to authority; for it is vain to make rules against sentiments . . . But if the Platonic bounds were transgressed, the offenders were deemed guilty of the worst species of bad form and at once became subject to criminal justice. At Clifton such transgressions were rare.

O.E. Christie's memories 1879–1885.

Victorian values?

Life in Clifton towards the end of the Victorian era had loosened up considerably: more fun was permissible, women had more freedom, discipline for the children was less harsh, and entertainment, at the Zoo, the circus, the Prince's Theatre, which had opened in 1867, or the Victoria Rooms, was plentiful and varied.

The growth of literacy brought about by the 1870 Education Act led to a proliferation of public and private libraries. By the 1880s Redland and Hotwells had public libraries (Clifton long resisted the idea as vulgar) and there were three private circulating libraries in Regent Street alone, including Massinghams with 50,000 volumes to lend. There was also at this time an amazing tally of booksellers in Clifton – 15 in all.

Clifton naturally had the most private subscribers when the telephone service arrived in Bristol.

The first experiment in local telephonic communication was in Clifton in 1877. As the *Bristol Times and Mirror* reported: "The telephone has been successfully tried from one part of the house of Dr. G.S. Thompson, Worcester Lawn, to another. A public exhibition of this useful invention will take place shortly at Bristol Museum."

By 1879 the system was running with 32 subscribers and shared lines, which won Bristol University College the chance to buy the land at the top of Park Street then occupied by the Blind School. Professor Alfred Marshall called the University number and overheard details of the planned sale.

In the early days there were no numbers and subscribers asked the exchange for the name of the person they wanted: the exchange operators had a code number for each and this became public knowledge. Early subscribers were Clifton Police station, whose number was 35, and Cordeux's, 108.

By 1880, the telephone cost £18 a year if you lived over half a mile from the exchange and £14.10s if you lived under half a mile. In June, 1881 a subsidiary exchange opened in Clifton at a private house, 27, Oakfield Grove to serve Clifton callers who by then numbered 135 out of the total Bristol directory – it was one page – of 637 subscribers.

Public call offices in Clifton, where you could use a business phone, arrived in 1886, and by 1894, there were 18 of them in the suburb. Clifton always believed in having the best modern contrivances and comforts.

The main problem was keeping all this wealth and jollity exclusive; from the early 1880s Cliftonians were fighting the public transport system which threatened to encroach into their suburb, bringing with it commercial ruin, noise and trippers. It must be stopped.

Trams up to this point went along Whiteladies Road only. There had been enough of a row letting the horse bus go past Cordeux's and through to the top of Sion Hill, and in the end, electric trams never came to Clifton.

Letters to the press shocked the rest of Bristol, so virulent was the tone. "Poor people do not walk about on Clifton streets, and now here are those money-making plebians of Bristol talking of running tramcars through our beautiful lordly Clifton! . . . why is this to be? Why must the common people be allowed to walk about here? They should stay in their own homes. They would feel more comfortable among their own houses and streets than here. The policemen should stop it", wrote one Disgusted in 1880. "Let them take the tram to Hotwells and then use the Lift" [The Rocks Railway].

"Is it not something terrible and most wicked that the disgusting tramway is to bring the nasty low inhabitants of Bristol up to our sacred region?" asked one writer, one hopes in parody. "We have nothing common or unclean among us at present."

There was a fear that "the sacred somnolence of Victoria Square may be destroyed." "Most visitors expect tranquillity and beauty in Clifton and will not find the tramways conducive to either." Trams would be ugly, noisy, would frighten the horses, metals in the road were dangerous to drive over and it lowered the tone.

In fact opinion was divided; some traders thought the tram would bring new custom to the village while others feared Cliftonians would use it to travel elsewhere to shop. It was a battle to be fought for decades: in the end Sir George White, chairman of the Tramway Company, bowed to Clifton grandees and gave up the idea of extending the trams to Clifton village.

There had even been agitation over the plan to have any transport on Sundays. It would, said

decent Clifton, entice young people into Sabbath-breaking. What they really feared was that hordes of humble clerks and labourers and their families would come to Clifton on their one day off and disport themselves on the sacred turf. "The Sunday cars will bring a vast number of people to the locality who have nothing in common with the residents who will so be driven to more peaceful retreats."

Meanwhile the common people down the hill at Hotwells had trams, but little else. Clifton continually tut-tutted about the state of their poor neighbours but what really shook Cliftonian complacency was a report on the Homes of the Bristol Poor, gathered by journalists on the *Times and Mirror* in 1884. The whole city was investigated, but the Hotwells reports, at the time of another slump in shipping, were unexpectedly shocking and embarrassing to Cliftonians because some of them were the owners and landlords.

The author wrote of "grandeur and decay at the Hotwells where once the stately houses of the wealthy and great are let out as tenements to families, the lets in one house [the Lebeck?] reaching 20, while in one nobly proportioned room where luxury formerly reigned supreme over a gay mansion full of light and music and high swelling hearts, we found last week a family in want of a bit of bread and one woman was sleeping on a sack on the bare floor.

"Within living memory carriages blocked the roads to the famous Gloucester Hotel on the occasion of a grand ball given in its stately assembly room. Now poverty-stricken people are receiving parish relief and are fighting the battle of life keenly for a crust of bread.

"One of the big houses, eight or ten roomed with central door and large hall, very faded outside, is let out in tenements. Twenty-six people live there: in one room a hobbler, wife and five children, one of whom is 18, and out of work for months, unable to pay 2s.6d a week rent. The mother and children chop sticks for firewood in a room about 20 feet square entirely without furniture except an old bedstead. They sold two cwt. of wood to raise 1s. 6d. and had only half a loaf between them – it was not living, it was lingering.

"In a dark court hemmed in with houses, a labourer who has only earned 7s. 5d. in seven weeks, pays 3s. a week for a three roomed house, bare because they have been selling things for food for

EXHIBITS AT THE CLIFTON INDUSTRIAL SHOW, 1881, held at the old Long Room.

Machines, models, handicrafts, carvings, needlework, knitting, cookery, stuffed birds, moths and butterflies, eggs, miscellaneous objects such as two model boots in wood, a lioness's skin, a walking stick made of Champagne corks, and a glass beehive.

ENTERTAINMENT, 1891

Mrs Shaw, the Whistling Lady, paid Clifton a second visit on December 2 and the interest aroused by her melodious warbling was shown by an audience which fairly filled the large hall at the Victoria Rooms.

Clifton Chronicle, **1891.**

CLIFTON CELEBRATES

Queen Victoria's Jubilee, June, 1887.
In the matter of decorations and illuminations, Clifton presented a very gay and festive appearance, the absence of any outward and visible sign of loyalty, even in the poorer districts, including the Hotwells, being the exception not the rule.
Verandahs in Caledonia Place were decorated with Chinese lanterns, festoons and flags; there were draped portraits, illuminated VR's, banners, globes with letters on them spelling out the name Victoria. Royal York Crescent was illuminated with 4,000 gas jets placed along the top of the railing, with 1,600 ft of piping. Rodney Place and Clifton College were illuminated on the old-fashioned plan which prevailed 50 years ago viz, placing candles in the different panes in all the windows.
The decorations in the Hotwells were chiefly confined to strings of flags suspended across the streets and displays of flags on poles projected from upper windows. A ball was given by the Mayor at the Victoria Rooms, there was a procession of school children and treats, a grand military review on Durdham Down and 3,000 aged poor of Clifton parish were entertained to dinner.

68. Pleasure steamers
brought a modest
revival of tourism to
Hotwells.

69. Hotwells families
relied on the working
docks for their
livelihood.

the six children and the wife who is expecting another."

A last ditch attempt to revive the Hotwell was made as late as 1886, without success since the area was in such decline – but there was eventually a solution: they pumped the water up to salubrious Clifton instead.

But the trouble was that anyone who tried to *change* Clifton was accused of inviting the undesirables in.

One of the most intriguing and secret buildings in Clifton is King's Arcade, or the Clifton Bazaar, in King's Road and Boyce's Avenue. At the time of writing it is up for sale yet again, for conversion into a modern arcade of boutiques – which was exactly its purpose when it was built in 1879. It was a Victorian version of the shopping mall.

The self-styled architect and entrepreneur was Joseph King, a builder who in 1873 built a row of Italianate shops in Whiteladies Road – it used to be occupied by the Alexandra – and a few houses such as Richmond Buildings, and 13–15 Clifton Road.

His grand scheme for Boyce's Avenue met, as always, with cries from the residents that it would attract undesirable characters from the city, but King went ahead anyway. He built two separate buildings, the shopping arcade itself, in King's Road (which he named) and at right angles to it, in Boyce's Avenue, a reception and entrance way to the arcade, with a space in the middle for carriages to drive inside the complex. (A single storey shop has been built in the gap, and the rest of the spaces in the street were later infilled)

In front of his arcade was a pleasure ground, matching the one already laid out in the front of Boyce's Buildings. According to a contemporary plan, the lawn had an entrance opposite Rodney Place, another in King's Road, and it had seven large trees standing where W.H. Smiths and the row of shops are now.

King's Clifton Bazaar and Winter Garden opened on April 7th, 1879. It was an instant flop – it became known as King's Folly and all Clifton said I told you so. His first advertisement in fact describes why: it was an over-ambitious speculation without tenants. King had hoped to let spaces in his arcade, as the ad explains, and only act as manager of the enterprise.

"Bristol and Clifton Bazaar and Winter Gardens now open. Situated near the Clifton Suspension Bridge and Downs, with Entrances in King's Road and Boyce's Avenue, Victoria Square.

"The Building, which is designed and erected by Mr Joseph William King of this city, at a cost of over £10,500, is very convenient and elegant in appearance, well-lighted, ventilated and heated with hot water and it is very commodious, having over 20,000 feet of floor space – and the glass roof and other parts of the Building are very artistically arranged with virgin cork, Ferns, creeping Plants and moss and to which will shortly be added tropical and other plants and shrubs, Fountains in play, Choice Fish, English and Foreign Birds etc., which will present a very cheerful and agreeable appearance.

"It has a GRAND RESTAURANT where refreshments may always be had at a low tariff. There are also Private Retiring Rooms and lavatories.

"A Choice Assortment of Flowers in Pots or cut for Bouquets always on sale.

"Spaces may be had for the Exhibition of Mechanical and other Modes.

"SHOPS to be LET with immediate possession, for Fancy Businesses. For particulars at the premises.

"A Celebration BAND is engaged to Play Every Saturday from three o'clock until 9pm.

"Open 9am–9pm. Joseph W. King FRHS, proprietor.

"Visitors to Bristol and Clifton should not fail to Visit the Winter Gardens for refreshments."

By December that year, it had failed and had become The Wilsonia Depot, selling magnetic belts, corsets, vests, spine bands and gloves. "Take medicine and Die, Apply Magnetic Currents and Live," they advertised.

This venture also failed and the Wilsonia sold out in January 1880 to Knee Brothers who needed a warehouse for their furniture storage business – there was already a Mrs Knee trading as a grocer in Boyce's Avenue and no doubt she tipped them off.

Knees, who were to keep the complex for over a century, advertised in 1880 that they had "purchased the premises known as the Winter Gardens and fitted them up as a Pantechnicon and is now open for the reception of furniture of every description. Separate rooms [King's intended boutiques] all heated by Hot Water, carriages warehoused or sold on commission, furniture bought sold or exchanged, household removals."

When they finally moved out in the 1980s, the whole arcade was found to be unsafe – King was not a very good builder! It is now about to see another rebirth.

VICTORIAN VALUES 1886

"The fact that a firm of contractors came to Bristol to engage 50 men at 17s. to 20s. per week and could only procure 37 speaks for itself. The ranks of the unemployed comprise very largely that numerous body who prefer charity to wages, indolence to honest labour and whose cry still is 'we want no work to do.'"

Letter from a Cliftonian about unemployment, 1886.

SERVANTS AT RISK, 1890

A Caution to Mistresses and Maids from the Ladies Association for the Care of Friendless Girls. "We should be thankful to be allowed to point out some ways in which young servants who (though possibly giddy and thoughtless) have no desire to do wrong, may be kept from falling prey to the many agents of evil who are ever on the watch to lay a snare for their feet.
1. Danger of leaving a single servant in charge of a house during the absence of the family.
2. We are most anxious to induce mistresses not to let young servants go out, especially on Bank Holidays, to places of amusement without enquiring the nature of the entertainment and the character of the companions who will accompany them.
3. Evil arises from mistresses allowing young servants too much liberty in the evenings or on Sundays. In some of the saddest cases, the mischief has originated (from sheer ignorance of danger) by accepting the invitation of a stranger and taking a walk after Sunday evening service. In one very painful case, the evil arose from the fact of a young and inexperienced servant girl being entrusted with a latch-key. If mistresses could see the depths to which girls often sink in consequence of one false step . . .

A DOCTOR WRITES

I am happy to say I have never vaccinated any person and am of the opinion that such a wicked and cruel and unnatural practice should be PROHIBITED by an Act of Parliament.

Clifton Chronicle, **1886.**

A CLIFTON FLOGGING SCANDAL

A small ad in *The Times*: "Intractable girls trained and educated, advice by letter 5s., Mrs. Walters, Bristol."
[Mrs. Eliza Walters was the widow of the former headmaster of All Saints School, lived at 53 Oakfield Road, and specialised in corporal punishment for girls whose parents were too cowardly to use it themselves]
A 1890s reporter posing as a prospective parent found "a tall strong woman arrayed in a dress of some sort of order and wearing a medallion of the Good Shepherd" who described how she strapped girls down on a table and administered strokes of the birch "to the orthodox surface."
"I measure my distance and proceed to strike slowly but firmly. By moving gently forward each stroke is differently placed and six strokes may be sufficient if well given with full force . . . for screams, increased strokes must be given." She charged half a guinea per treatment or £100 a year, and more for girls over 20, and appeared to enjoy her work, for she had a full engagement book.

THE GENTLEMANLY YOUNG LADY

In my young days, young ladies were admired and courteously treated by the opposite sex because they were MAIDENLY. This in no way prevented them being intellectual, they were companions for men but did not attempt as now to do all a man does. I see girls now assuming a more than manly stride, walking with sticks, standing in manly attitudes, riding bicycles, playing cricket, golf, football, but in all these girls there is a lack of modesty and in some I might even say decency. Today unblushingly, these girls put on the divided skirt, some wear knicker-bockers; they look with scorn upon the graceful folds of drapery which should adorn a woman's figure. I ask myself what sort of wives these girls make? They will be the ruin of the home life of England.

A Lover of Modesty, on the girl of the present period.
Clifton Chronicle, **1886.**

70. Joseph King's unsuccessful Victorian shopping arcade in Boyce's Avenue.

71. & 72. Shops lining the Hotwell Road in the 1880s and 'quality' Park Street where every shop had its sunblind.

73. Not just animals: Clifton Zoo as funfair.

It was publisher and MP George Newnes who eventually provided Clifton with the boost it was looking for.

He obviously knew Clifton, was interested in investment and engineering projects and undertook to build a railway through the rock from the Hotwell to Clifton and to establish a new hydropathic hotel next door.

There was an interesting subtext: the Rocks Railway was needed to bring visitors up from the Hotwells railway and tram terminus precisely because Clifton itself refused to let a tram service into its august precincts. The Tramway Company had suggested an exterior railway up the rock but the Merchant Venturers had turned it down because it would look unsightly.

An added advantage of any scheme was that the domestic servants who came from Hotwells, and so did not usually live in, could get to work more easily, if their employers paid the penny up – but not of course the halfpenny down, for servants could walk.

Boring of the steep shaft began in March 1891: it was to be 500 feet long, 18 foot high and lit by gas and daylight. It was a difficult project, bedevilled by rockfalls and eventually cost three times the estimated figure.

The design was for an interior funicular railway, with four cars in two pairs, each seating 18 passengers, and would be powered by gravity and water. Beneath each passenger section was a tank, and water was pumped in and out according to the number of users. The cars were light blue and white with gold lines, and the interior was lit by oil lamps.

The actual opening on March 12th, 1893 took Clifton by surprise and only a dozen or so people

74. En route to Clifton: the Hotwells tram links with the Rocks Railway.

75. The Clifton Pump Room, opened in 1894, later became a cinema and ballroom.

STATION: BRISTOL. POSTAL ADDRESS: CRAWFORD, CLIFTON. TELEGRAMS: "COACHING, BRISTOL."

WYKEHAM HOUSE,
MANILLA ROAD, CLIFTON.

Among the Public Schools at which Pupils of Mr. CRAWFORD's have been previously educated, are the following:—ETON, HARROW, DULWICH, CHARTERHOUSE, MARLBOROUGH, RUGBY, CLIFTON, WELLINGTON, ROSSALL, BATH, CHELTENHAM, MALVERN.

MR. G. E. CRAWFORD, M.A.,
13th WRANGLER,

Late Classical Scholar of Brasenose College, Oxford; late Foundation Scholar for Mathematics of Trinity College, Cambridge; Vidil Prizeman for French, and First Prizeman for an English Declamation; for some time Assistant Master at Harrow,

Personally prepares Pupils, with the assistance of a large Staff of experienced Tutors, Graduates of their respective Universities, for

ALL EXAMINATIONS,
AND IN PARTICULAR FOR

*INDIAN, CEYLON, AND HOME CIVIL SERVICES,
INDIAN WOODS AND FORESTS, AND DIPLOMATIC APPOINTMENTS,

*WOOLWICH,	OXFORD RESPONSIONS,	*CAMBRIDGE PREVIOUS,
*SANDHURST,	*OXFORD PASS GREATS,	*CAMBRIDGE GENERAL,
*MILITIA LITERARY,	*OXFORD HONOURS GREATS,	MATHEMATICAL TRIPOS,
*COOPER'S HILL,	*LONDON MATRICULATION,	LAW PRELIMINARY,
	*COLLEGE OF PRECEPTORS.	

* Pupils are *actually being prepared*, as this sheet goes through the press, either singly or in small Classes suitably arranged, for all of the eleven different Examinations marked with an asterisk (*). It is believed that this achievement is unsurpassed in the West of England, and probably anywhere out of London.

[*See also page* 19A.]

CLARENDON COLLEGIATE SCHOOL
(FOR LADIES),
155 Whiteladies Road, Clifton, Bristol.

PRINCIPAL: MRS. MAYNARD.   HEAD MISTRESS: MISS MAYNARD.

(Assisted by Highly Qualified and Certificated Governesses and Masters.)

During the past three years more than 80 Pupils have passed the University Local College of Preceptors, and Music Examinations. One was First in all England in French and German. Patent hygienic chair-desks are used in the class rooms. Small classes. Individual teaching. Ambulance and Cookery Lectures. Needle-work.

MUSIC TAUGHT ON THE GERMAN SYSTEM THROUGHOUT THE SCHOOL.
Ages of Pupils: SEVEN TO TWENTY-ONE; *Average number per term:* FORTY.

BRISTOL NURSES' TRAINING INSTITUTION AND HOME,
23 & 24, RICHMOND TERRACE, CLIFTON.
ESTABLISHED 31 YEARS.

Trained Medical, Surgical, Monthly, and Mental Nurses supplied; also experienced Masseuse. Patients received in the Home for Surgical Treatment, from £4 4s. per week.

Address: "LADY SUPERINTENDENT." Telegrams: "NURSES BRISTOL." Telephone No. 555.

were there to see the first car ascend, after a few hitches. Over 6,000 persons used the lift as it came to be called, on that first day, and "many paid double fare to secure a pleasing little memento of the occasion, a gilded Maltese cross bearing a representation of the lift, the initials of the promoter, and the inscription CRR, commenced 1881, completed 1893."

During the first 12 months 427,492 passengers were carried and there was no accident of any kind. On Bank Holidays 1,000 passengers an hour used it and the nervous were reassured: "The cars cannot run down the incline by themselves and if left untouched even after they have started on their journey, *THEY WILL STOP PERFECTLY STILL* gripping the rails with a tremendous vice-like tenacity."

In the end it had a comparatively short life: the company went into receivership in 1908 and the Tramways Company bought it, but eventually the arrival of the motor car and the Portway finished it off. It closed in 1934.

The next stage in Newnes' plan was the hotel, at first known as the Clifton Grand Spa and Hydro, or the Clifton Pump Room. It was to be formed by buying up and reconstructing the three end houses in Prince's Buildings, and water for the hydro was to be pumped up from the Hotwell spring below.

The Pump Room itself, the remains of which await restoration at the time of writing, opened in 1894, but plans were not carried out according to the elegant design "owing to the self-seeking opposition of an individual," says Latimer mysteriously.

A set of marble baths reached by a 100 ft marble corridor were planned for a lower site to be excavated from the rock, and there were elaborate schemes for ornamental gardens sloping down to the water, with tennis lawns, conservatories, a vinery, a teahouse overhanging the river, alcoves, a terrace, and walled gardens. The hotel company seems to have purchased the Colonnade as part of its scheme. These plans were never realised, though early photographs of the hotel do show terracing, greenhouses and gardens instead of the scrub that now exists.

What did open was a one storey building containing the Pump Room with "four ornamental dolphins who hold in their mouths the silver taps from which the mineral water is drawn, the dolphins supporting a water nymph upholding a seashell from which a spray of water is constantly playing."

"A marble staircase leading from the entrance in Sion Hill has at its foot gentlemen's lavatories beautifully fitted having marble dados and mosaic floors. The two retiring rooms have stained glass and marble statuary. The Pump Room is a handsome appartment 100 ft, long and 58 ft, wide a particular feature being 20 huge monolithic columns in Cipolline marble."

The actual hotel did not open until March 1898 with a grand reception for nearly 700 guests, the Band of the Life Guards and vocalist Madame Jeannie Strathearn; it was the hotel rather than the Pump Room which was a success, for the spa movement was over. In 1920 the Pump Room was turned into a cinema and later a dance hall.

The century was almost done and Clifton still thought of itself as a holiday resort rather than a suburb of Bristol; the Clifton and Hotwells Improvement Association advertised the charms of Clifton in Indian newspapers. But in reality, the resort days were over, along with the century and the reign of Queen Victoria.

ZOO LARKS, 1893

I went to the stage and found a performance was going on. There were comedians, nice tarts singing and dancing, one with an Ally Sloper baby in her arms, another was dressed like a black negro queen in short skirt and headdress of feathers. Then a fellow came on playing musical instruments, mandolin, bells, harp etc. Next a big overgrown schoolboy in mortar board, jacket and collar, doing a lot of larking. It was a puzzle how they done it. Next there was a little fellow performing tricks on a bicycle, dressed like an 11th hussar he mounts his bicycle and makes a grand charge.

I went round by the lake and seen a man climb up on a wire over the water. With pole in hand, he walked along it and either by accident or design tumbled off. Then I goes touring all the houses seeing the various animals. I strolls about, had smokes, and a lot of nice dotlets were dancing to the band, playing kiss in the ring. When it got dark they had displays of fireworks and sent up a balloon.

From 'A Holiday Fete At The Zoo Gardens, Clifton, August 8, 1893,' from the *Diary of a Bristolian*, by W.H. Bow.

LETTER TO THE EDITOR FROM DISGUSTED OF CLIFTON, 1889

Salvation Army Collections. "A Major visited about 50 houses in wealthy Clifton and the result of his labours was one shilling."

Letter, *Clifton Chronicle*, 1889.

ALCOHOL ON SALE AT THE ZOO

My attention was drawn to the boisterous behaviour of both girls and boys. The girls seemed the worst. I have seen rough behaviour at fairs but never saw among women such horrible behaviour. In my experience as a medical man I could see they were drunk. Some of the girls were reeling drunk and seemed unable to rise from the seats.

Letter to *Western Daily Press*, from Dr. Thomas Webster, 1881.

PLUS ÇA CHANGE
A letter on the state of Princes Victoria Street.

It is discreditable that a main road leading from Regent Street to Princes Buildings should be allowed to remain in the condition it is and has been for years. From Messrs Lewis [now Tyndall's Bank] to the end are a series of stables with coach houses having double doors opening outwards across the pavement so that passers-by have to take to the road whatever condition it may be in. The condition of the roadway is, to use a very mild term, most disreputable and from a want of repair dangerous to vehicular traffic. The whole of the road from the Mall is a continuance of ruts and channel course. On the left hand side from Princes Buildings, it commences with six or eight decent dwellings and then you may imagine a settlement of squatters, for its inhabitants are cocks and hens and a few ducks disporting themselves in the public road. They come from shanties at the back of Caledonia Place. At intervals the walls have given way and tons of earth and stones have fallen into the road. There is no footpath on this side of the road until you reach the beer house [Seconds]. The houses at the end are not numbered, the lighting is imperfect and the constabulary are conspicuous by their absence.

***Clifton Chronicle*, 1886.**

AMUSEMENT FOR THE WORKING CLASSES

The Committee are in a position to offer great variety of amusement for the Working classes Viz one splendid Billiard table full-sized and one smaller table, also other games such as Chess, Draughts, Dominoes etc. The Committee have also introduced a Musical Evening once a week for the benefit of young members as an inducement to join the club without having to seek amusement at the public house. Gambling is strictly forbidden.

Description of the Clifton Working Men's Club and Institute, opened in Victoria Street, 1884. [It was about where Seconds is now]

DILAPIDATION IN THE VICTORIA ROOMS

In the small room, if one sits on a seat near the wall, one is in constant dread of a piece of beading just hanging loosely on the wall falling onto one's head. In the seats at the back the rush bottoms have gone, the whole room presents an air of dismall decay, ceilings discoloured by damp, gas jets four out of ten with the glasses broken and gone and those remaining filled with the dirt of ages. Surely such a state of things is a disgrace to Clifton.

Letter to *Clifton Chronicle*, 1885.

AN AESTHETIC BALL AT THE VICTORIA ROOMS, JANUARY 1886

Given by Mrs James Lyon, wealthy widow of 26, Victoria Square.

It was a fashionable reunion which may be regarded as the ball of the season, and attended by all the elite of Clifton. 400 invitations were sent from the Mayor down. Mrs Lyon, elegantly attired in a train of black and gold velvet brocade with a petticoat of old gold satin covered with black Brussels lace, her ornaments being diamonds, received with her daughter in the Victoria Rooms, transformed by Messrs Gane and Trapnell, furnishers of College Green.

The whole suite of rooms was engaged for the occasion and done up in the aesthetic manner. The octagon was fitted up as a drawing room with cabinets and seats in the Chippendale style in the recesses, portières over the doors of peacock pattern tapestry bordered with black velvet and sunflower ornaments; in the angles of the room were blue and white vases of true aesthetic type filled with sunflowers and amaryllis lilies.

The large salon used as a ballroom was fitted up in a most brilliant manner with a dado of dark coloured cloth over which was a panelling of peacock green embroidered with flowers. In the larger windows were gilded moresque panels of tracery in front of which were hung large brackets holding azaleas and dracenas; between the windows were immense mirrors draped with rich satin plush and lace. Round the galleries were festoons of roses and other bright flowers and between these etageres were suspended some superb Florentine glasses set in rich velvet. Immense silvered globes were suspended under the end gallery.

All was simplicity and elegance and refinement. Dancing commenced at 9 pm (21 dances) and was kept up with great spirit until an early hour, indeed the tout ensemble of the ballroom when lighted up presented a picture of animation and beauty which has not been seen in Clifton for very many years.

The Supper Menu was: Saumon à la Royale. Game Pies, Boar's Head, Tongues. Turkey a la Royal. Ham. Roast Turkeys. Mayonnaise de Homard. Filets de Sole en Aspic. Raised peafowl pie. Lamb cutlets en Aspic. Plovers and snipe. Black game. Raised pigeon pie. Pâté de fois gras en Aspic. Rouelle de veau. Roast Chickens. Aspic de petits Oiseaux. Gallantine de poulets. Beouf bouilli aux naturel. Victoria cake. Savoury cake. Compôte de fruits. Maraschino Bavarian cream. Swiss Ice Pudding. Wine jelly. Noyeau jelly. Lemon Cream. Maraschino jelly. Trifles. Compôte d'oranges. Genoese pastry. Charlotte Russe. Vanilla Cream. Pineapple Cream. French pastry. Maids of Honour. [Afterwards they might well have needed Cockle's Anti-Bilious Pills, 1s. a box]

MEAN AND SQUALID

The greater portion of the Hotwells is anything but salubrious or fashionable; the road by which trams approach the foot of the Suspension Bridge being particularly mean and squalid; the busy fingers of commerce have metamorphosed the scene but the locality being at such a low level, its decadence in no ways affects the reputation or beauty of Clifton.

From *Where to Buy in Bristol and Clifton*. 1890.

WOMEN'S PROBLEMS

WOMEN who have been deceived by the misleading advertisements, testimonials, and other worthless representations of Madames, Nurses, companies, doctors' widows etc, should send a stamped addressed envelope for my little book which tells you why these people fail to cure you. It explains in a scientific way HOW REGULARITY MAY BE RESTORED in a few hours without discomfort. . . .

96

76. St Vincent's Rocks Hotel with the Sion Spring bath house in its original state.

77. These Clifton children at 30 Cornwallis Crescent were to see immense change as the new century progressed.

Change and decay

"Signs of mourning are universal," observed the *Clifton Chronicle*, printed with thick black borders on every page, on January 30th, 1901. "Every social function has been abandoned and numerous events postponed."

The death of Queen Victoria had a terrific impact; packed churches were draped in black, and congregations all dressed in deep mourning heard special sermons – the text at Hope Chapel was Mark ch XIV, v. 8. "She hath done what she could."

Wreaths were placed on her statue on College Green, and business was practically suspended in Clifton on the day of the funeral, Saturday February 2nd, when the *Chronicle* reported that nearly every person met on the streets was attired in mourning. Muffled bells were rung and in Mr Bromhead's window in Regent Street, photographs of floral tributes sent to Windsor by Clifton College and the University went on show.

All transport stopped for five minutes at the time of the funeral and Rose Lillian Williams of Clifton wrote a little poem:

A wail of sorrow and a burst of song,
And then a silence tender as a tear.
Leave her, lov'd Queen, to her cherished rest.

Things were not to be the same again in suburbs such as Clifton: although the style of King Edward VII seemed to indicate that life would be as before, Clifton was beginning to show cracks in its social fabric.

In the actual fabric, too. The big old Georgian houses were now unfashionable, and too big for one family to run. The 1870 Education Act bringing compulsory schooling had had its effect and working class girls had other options than becoming servants. So the smaller more modern late Victorian villa became more attractive, especially in plumbing terms, than a Georgian terrace house, and these began to be dwindle into apartment and lodging houses.

(Until after World War I, it was considered improper for spinsters to live in flats; they lived in boarding houses, as did bachelors, while the poor lived in tenements, ie big houses divided into one or two room apartments)

The Builder editorialised: "We view with amazement the operation of the speculative builders in Clifton who are engaged in erecting with military precision enormous ranges of terrace houses in stone and stucco and wonder if these enterprising men will stand the financial strain or figure next in the list of bankrupts."

The result was a worrying number of void properties in old Clifton, with estate agents' notices everywhere and an air of desperation. "House agents tell us that if owners of local property could only modernise and abolish those dreadful basements which servants fight shy of – there would be few voids in Clifton. A fortune is waiting the man who would erect a number of modern houses at rentals of between £40 and £50 a year," wrote one concerned citizen in 1906.

Yet the idea persisted that Clifton was the only socially correct place to live. When Professor Arthur Tyndall of the University Physics department married in 1908, he and his wife planned to leave Clifton where all University staff were expected to live, and rent a house in Cotham.

"Whereupon two of my professional colleagues came to me and urged me to give up the idea. They told me that if I went the wrong side of Whiteladies Road, no-one would call on my wife. However we persisted in going to Cotham, fortunately without the dire consequences that were anticipated."

Keeping Clifton exclusive was hard work. The rearguard action against the trams went on. "It is tolerably certain that a large proportion of Clifton residents are of the well-to-do commercial class, some of whom retired from trade and some who live in Clifton with their families to escape at least a portion of the noise and turmoil of city life. Then there are the professional people and the vast number engaged in educational and other intellectual pursuits to whom the sanctity of quietude is all important, and they do not want Clifton, with its picturesque and peculiar environment as a residential suburb over-run by the multitude."

The battle over public transport being allowed into Clifton village actually continued until 1903. "We want carriages here not noisy electric cars. Let us do all we can to raise the tone of Clifton, not lower it." "If I were to learn that trams were presently to pass my door I would sell my house with the least possible delay."

78. By the end of the nineteenth century, speculative builders had changed the face of rural Clifton.

79. Bristol's first motor bus service ran from the Victoria Rooms to the Suspension Bridge from 1906. This bus is passing Cordeux's Store in Merchant's Road.

"Electric cars would bring people to Clifton perhaps, but what sort of people? Penny trampers are no use to Clifton, they will not fill our empty houses. By all means let them enjoy the pleasures of the Downs in common with ourselves. No-one would wish to deny them that."

"Numerous people come to Clifton for rest and quietness and I feel sure that we would lose many of this class if the electric cars were introduced and the swarms of people they could bring from the city."

Rest and quietness were not what the suffragettes were providing. Some of the Clifton ladies were disturbing the social fabric too.

The suffragists who deplored violent means held constant meetings and debates ("we are not peers and we are not lunatics, but still we are disenfranchised!") and put on suffrage plays like *The Typist*, and *Man And Woman*, at the All Saints Hall in Merchants Road.

For the militants, Mrs. Pethick Lawrence and Christabel Pankhurst came to the Victoria Rooms in November 1907, where the organisers hired a boxer to bounce out heckling medical students.

Even here people knew their place, according to the *Chronicle*. "In the front seats we noticed many leaders of Clifton society and at the back there were working women, among the latter being several factory operatives."

There was a mass rally on the Downs in September 1908, when "wholesale conversions were made. The demonstration attracted a crowd of 10,000, with seven speakers' platforms. It was an animated scene, with heated discussions. At one time groups of noisy youths did their best to cause a diversion, their favourite heckling trick being to ring a dinner bell to drown the speaker. There were cries of 'Go home and do the washing!'"

In 1909, Theresa Garnett who lived at 5, York Place, became nationally famous for attacking Winston Churchill with a dogwhip, on Temple Meads station. They called her St. Theresa after she cried "take that for the women of England," because Churchill was opposing votes for women. She was sent to Holloway prison where she joined

80. Theresa Garnett of Clifton. the suffragette who went to gaol for striking Winston Churchill with a dog whip.

Mrs Dove Willcox and May Allen, Clifton ladies both, and all three went on hunger strike and were forcibly fed.

They were recorded a "right royal reception" when they were released and came home: a procession met them at Temple Meads, with a military band and carriages decorated in the white green and purple colours of the movement, to escort them back to Clifton. That year Clifton got its first woman councillor, Emily Harriet Smith.

Suffragette activity came to a peak in 1913, when a group of them burned down the University's sports pavilion at Coombe Dingle, on October 23rd. "A clue to the authors of this outrage was provided by the message on a black-edged envelope attached to a suffragette paper, 'Business before pleasure.' On the verandah was found a can which had contained oil. The upper floor was utterly destroyed and the floor fell in. Outside the pavilion, a little hammer – a mere toy – was found."

Revenge by the students was swift. On October 24th at 5p.m. 400 or 500 of them rushed over to the suffragettes' headquarters, opposite the Museum and now occupied by Leokadia, and smashed the plate glass front with bricks, threw out the contents and set fire to them. (The shop's present upper window is different from its neighbours precisely because of this incident)

But a war of a different kind was to occupy the students and the suffragettes the following year.

When war broke out the *Chronicle* quickly urged Cliftonians not to pay the "inflated prices which certain purveyors of foodstuffs were attempting to extort from their customers under plea of war."

Nevertheless prudent householders sent their servants out to the shops to stock up. (Later on hoarding became illegal) Maximum prices were set: sugar 4d. a lb, butter 1s.6d., colonial cheese 9d. lard 8d., bacon 1s.4d. and margarine 10d.

Clifton went on a war footing; two houses at 6 and 9 Victoria Square were taken over to house Belgian refugees and an appeal went for furniture and clothing; 50 refugees arrived in September.

There were hurried wartime marriages, including one which went quite unremarked by society. On December 24th, 1914, at Emmanuel Church, Clifton, Agatha Mary Clarissa Miller, spinster aged 24, married Royal Flying Corps officer Archibald Christie of Olden Lodge, Guthrie Road.

The uniformed VAD members of the Clifton War Hospital Supply depot began to wind bandages and make dressings in the rooms above Cordeux's old store, and gradually the published list of Old Cliftonians killed in action grew longer and longer.

The war memorial at Clifton College, alma mater of General Haig who was leading the glorious defeat, contains 578 names; the school provided one Commander-in-Chief, one Commander, 23 Major-Generals, 52 Brigadier-Generals, and one VC, Comdr. Claude Congreve Dobson, RN, of 16, College Road.

The Zoo became the focus of entertainments for convalescent soldiers, 32,450 of them by the end of the war, and Clifton ladies provided them with tea and sympathy, three times a week. "Many friendships were formed and in some instances were the prelude to something stronger."

On American Independence Day, 1918, US servicemen were entertained at the Zoo, and on embarkation day when they went home in December, all day long lines of military vehicles crossed the Downs on the way to Avonmouth.

War changed everything and everybody, got women the vote, and got them to work.

81. & 82. Retribution: the University sports pavilion at Coombe Dingle burned down by suffragettes in October 1913. *Below*: the male students' revenge: destruction of the suffragettes' headquarters on the corner of Berkeley Square.

With men at war women had to take their place and even Clifton ladies began to take employment for the first time in their lives. In 1916, women were allowed to work on the trams, and by 1917 there were 800 women taking men's jobs. Shops hours were shortened to make it safe for women assistants to go home at night. There was the scandal of girls who "lost their heads and forced their attentions on soldiers in the streets and parks."

Feeding the family became difficult – the diet and the food shortages were far worse in the first war than in the second. There were food restrictions on meals in public, Wednesdays became meatless days and signs went up in Clifton stores like Shirleys, the high class grocer who had a business where Focus trades today, saying no butter, bacon, marg or cheese. Prices went up and quality, particularly of flour, went down.

There was a large demand for white bread instead of the usual wholemeal, and grumbles that women with children or babies got precedence in the queue. The shrewd ones "borrowed" a baby to go shopping.

In Hotwells an already poor diet became worse and in 1914 the schools medical officer reported that only 31% of schoolchildren were "perfect in health." Rickets, anaemia, TB and bronchial troubles were rife and at the end of the war, 785 Bristol children had TB, a fair number of them coming from Hotwells.

People did try to grow their own food: tennis courts and cricket pitches in Clifton were commandeered for allotments, and householders had to do the digging themselves as the servants had left to join the war effort.

Wartime privation increased the need for entertainment, to keep up morale, and the cinema could not have arrived at a better time.

The Triangle Cinema was the first: it was a former skating rink opened in 1909 by Emmanuel Harris. He converted it into a cinema in 1914: it had a spherical frontage and a pillared entrance, and inside a balcony, wide comfortable seats, a café with the screen visible from the tables, where lobster and tomato sandwiches were served. Harris was aiming at a rich clientèle so he engaged a fine orchestra, conducted by Clifton College's music master Maurice Alexander, to play suitable classics to accompany the silent films. A two and a half hour show cost 6d and members of the Fry and Cadbury families would roll up in their limousines. The building was lost in the Blitz.

83. & 84. Agatha Christie and opposite: certificate showing her marriage to Captain Christie at Emmanuel Church, Clifton.

Hotwells' own silent cinema can hardly have been so luxurious. It was two doors down from the Spring Gardens and it opened on November 29th, 1915. "Quite a large number of residents accepted invitations to an inauguration ceremony. The cinema has been erected by the Hotwells Cinema Co, of which Mr W.J. Haynes is secretary and licencee," said the *Chronicle*. Miss Viola Jukes, who lived in a basement in Dowry Square, was the pianist and singer.

"The building is substantial, lofty and spacious. There are two spacious entrances and no fewer than five exits so that the place can be emptied in two minutes. The building is carpeted throughout in luxurious style, there is sitting accommodation for about 450 persons in tip-up chairs upholstered in red velvet. There are two Gaumont machines and performances daily 6.30–10.30 pm, and Saturday afternoons for children. Prices 3d., 4d. and 6d."

It even opened on Christmas Day with a showing of *The Canker Of Jealousy, A Domestic Drama*. Silent film captions revealed the illiteracy among the older Hotwells generation who missed compulsory schooling: one Hotwells pensioner remembers her father paying for local children to come in with him so that they could read the captions aloud for him.

Soon Cliftonians could also see films at the Victoria Rooms or the Coliseum, another former skating rink, or the Clifton Pump Room, whose hydropathic ambitions had not been realised.

But by the end of the war everyone was weary and depressed; when Armistice Day finally came it was not a moment too soon.

Post-war Clifton tried hard to shake off the gloom – but there were so many young men dead, so many widows and spinsters living alone in reduced

circumstances. It was a world Clifton novelist E.H. Young understood, for she too was made a widow by the war: her solicitor husband Arthur, who had supported her suffragette activities, and shared her love of amateur dramatics – actress Gladys Young was her sister – died at Ypres in 1917. During the war she had worked in a munitions factory and as a groom at a local stables.

Emily Young came from Northumberland and in 1902, at the age of 22, married Arthur Daniell, member of a respected Bristol legal family. From 1907 until Arthur's death, they lived in the top floor flat at 2, Saville Place. She began to observe Clifton residents and their social habits with a humorous and sharp eye. She must also have roamed every lane and alley and terrace of her new home, because her seven books set in Upper Radstowe as she calls Clifton, are so accurate that you know exactly where her characters are walking and even which house they live in.

She captures perfectly the social pretentions, the rules and conventions of polite society and the penalties that those who don't observe them must pay. She charts the sad and seedy hinterland that single people in reduced circumstances experience living in lodgings and ridicules gently the power of the clergy and the big house.

And you can also appreciate the misleading surface of Clifton life from E.H. Young's own

LORD HAIG AT CLIFTON COLLEGE

85. Preparing for war: Ex-Cliftonian Lord Haig inspecting college cadets.

subsequent romantic career: after being widowed, she went to live with a Bristol Grammar School friend of her husband's, Ralph Henderson, and his wife, in a ménage à trois. He was headmaster of a famous school, Alleyn's, but not a breath of scandal emerged. Yet from the chronology it is perfectly clear that Emily Young and Ralph Henderson's liaison began before her husband died. And Clifton didn't find out.

The liberal Daniell family was in fact used to scandal: Miriam Daniell, Arthur's artist aunt, an early Bristol socialist and suffragette, left her husband in Clifton to live openly in a lesbian relationship in working class St. Philip's. This was also the family that entertained artist Stanley Spencer at their soirées in 1915.

Spencer was then working as a medical orderly at the Beaufort Hospital, now Glenside, and his great friend was the artistic and literary Desmond Macready Chute, of the actor manager family who ran the Theatre Royal and the Prince's.

Chute carried him off to his Clifton home at Tyndall's Park and in Spencer's off duty time the unlikely pair explored Clifton and Chute introduced him to all his friends, and the Clifton hostesses of the day.

Spencer wrote "I go down to Mrs Daniell's to hear some singing on my half-days. Mrs Daniell has a fine voice and so has her daughter. I felt quite crackey with delight to hear some duets out of *Figaro* and they sang them well. . . . I shall always be grateful to Mrs Daniell."

No sooner had Clifton recovered from the war years than the economy began to slide. Clifton felt its effects gradually, but the impact in Hotwells was far worse.

Hotwells had had a brief boom in the 1880s and 1890s, when the street was widened and shops lined both sides from end to end, and immediately after the First World War Hotwells thrived, because the war had stimulated industry and the Port of Bristol was busy – now that the Hotwell itself was well and

106

A KHAKI WEDDING 1916

Miss Mary Hunford Jones of Oakfield Road and Capt F. Birkett of the Queen's Royal West Surrey Regiment at Christchurch, Clifton. The bride's dress was of khaki honeycomb cloth trimmed with skink, nigger brown velvet hat trimmed with silk and veil to match and she carried a shower bouquet of white carnations and lilies tied with the colours of the Queen's Regiment. The bridesmaids wore French gray cashmere.

The groom, who was educated at Monkton Combe School, joined his battalion in France in December 1914 and was slightly wounded in the arm. He rejoined and was dangerously wounded in both legs in May 1916, brought home and made a slow recovery.

Clifton Chronicle, **January 1916.**

THE TONE OF THE PICTURE HOUSE

We believe picture houses have a very useful part to play in the life of our times. To them when the day's work is done men take their wives and families and for an astonishingly small sum spend a pleasant evening out of the cold and the rain in the company of their fellow men. Here is an opportunity of providing amusement without coarseness and vulgarity.

Letter, *Clifton Chronicle*, **1916.**

ARMISTICE DAY IN CLIFTON,
November 11, 1918

A sullen morning, business as usual, little groups stood near the newspaper offices – the news spread rapidly. Busy city men stopped passers-by; shop-keepers and assistants rushed eagerly into the street; church bells rang out. A holiday spirit developed, flags, cheers, ribbons, music, processions of vehicles. Ragamuffins without boots began beating tin cans, sang war songs. A procession of students in gowns formed, US soldiers danced in the street. A half holiday was declared at Clifton College and a telegram sent to Field Marshal Haig.

Clifton Chronicle.

CLIFTON IN 1918

After the Armistice, Clifton life continued to flow in its spacious channels. Literary and other groups met to talk about books, to listen to good music, to paint or discuss works of art. The Clifton dinner party was a true mirror of the 19th century and from time to time gatherings took place reminiscent of the routs of a still earlier time.

But some of the magnificence was already becoming a little faded and the glory was departing. Old Clifton families increasingly preferred a villa in Stoke Bishop or a home in the country, while the fair mansions were turned into flats or allowed to degenerate into tenements.

Professor C.M. MacInnes.

HOTWELLS IN THE THIRTIES

On Saturday night, from 6p.m. onwards, Trinity to the Mardyke was really busy with people shopping up to 10 p.m. Everyone lived on the premises and people knocked on the door if they wanted anything. They sent their kids with a note 'Let Dolly have 2ozs. ham and four rashers of bacon, pay you tomorrow'.

Christmas Eve it would be near midnight when you closed. You could buy everything you needed from the cradle to the grave – baby clothes, wedding dresses and coffins. There was a cinema, a Chinese laundry, and you could hire a handcart to fetch coke from the gasworks.

ARTY FOLK

Clifton Arts Club in the 1930s met on Saturday afternoons in a tall Georgian house just off Park Street. The owner, Miss Methven Brownlee always wore a wide brimmed hat and a brown cloak and smoked innumerable cigarettes in a long holder. Painters, musicians, writers were among the membership, which included Douglas Cleverdon who had opened a bookshop a few yards up the road. He persuaded Eric Gill to design the fascia. The Arts Club ended when a 1940 bomb demolished the house and killed the owner.

Anne Edbrooke-Ballard.

DISGUSTED WRITES AGAIN, 1900s

To the shopowners of Clifton – why do Clifton shop-owners stand alone in all England in regard to the early closing movement and not close at 2 p.m. on Wednesdays?

Clifton Chronicle, **1900.**

May I through your columns make a most decided and earnest protest against the commencement of Sunday omnibus traffic in this part of Clifton. Clifton has so long been famed for its quiet and orderly Sunday. Have the directors of the Omnibus Company no consideration for their horses or their men?

1901.

A REVOLVER IN CLIFTON, 1906

A gentleman named John Whitemore, 37, on a visit to Clifton, pointed a loaded revolver at James Jolly, licencee of the Richmond Springs Hotel, Gordon Road. At 10.15 pm, he entered the complainant's house and ordered two glasses of beer. He asked the landlord if he wasn't a Scotchman and abused him. At last he was so troublesome he was ordered out and he then presented a six-chambered loaded revolver.

A GRAND BAZAAR at the Victoria Rooms, 1901

A Grand Bazaar with a set of BEAUTIFUL LIVING PICTURES (beautifully lit by coloured electric lamps) will (DV) be given by the Church of St. Paul, Clifton, on behalf of the new church of the poor parish of St. Michael and All Angels, Bedminster, in the Victoria Rooms. The opening ceremony by the Lady Doreen Long is on October 17 and until October 19 there will be concerts, a conjurer, dramatic performances, a Professor of Phrenology, Mandoline Band, shooting gallery, picturesque stalls, and Good Refreshments.

CRIME IN HOTWELLS

"A shocking scene was enacted at a house in Dowry Square. It appears that number 8, like many of the large old houses in the neighbourhood, is let out in tenements and that the back two rooms were occupied by a Mr and Mrs Prosser. The landlord considered them a respectable couple and the man was employed in building operations as a carpenter. During the holidays the other occupants of the house were disturbed by noise and quarrelling. About 5a.m. they were alarmed by the screams of Mrs Prosser and the landlord who lives in the Polygon was called to gain admission: Prosser, with a hatchet in his hand, was in the act of striking his wife who lay on the floor her head bleeding profusely. . . ."

Clifton Chronicle, **1906.**

PALMISTRY IN CLIFTON, 1902

At the Bristol Police Court Edward Simmons who described himself as Professor Ramases, of 21 Regent Street Clifton, was charged with unlawfully using subtle crafts, means and devices to deceive or impose upon certain subjects of H.M. the King. Fined £5 for reading the palms of two women who paid 1s 6d. each.

Clifton Chronicle, **1906.**

MAD SPEED IN CLIFTON

P.C. Roscow who had been forced to jump out of the way when the car shot out at a junction, said he had been in the district for 15 years and he had never seen a car go so fast before. The defendant, Charles Henry Richards of 21, Pembroke Road, a well-known citizen, had been a motorist for 13 or 14 years. The car was built in 1907 and the older a car was, the more noise it made. "At no point was the car going at more than 10 or 12 mph," he said. Fined £10 and 2gns costs.

Clifton Chronicle, **1913.**

truly finished, the docks were the economic mainstay of the district.

Then came the slump of the late Twenties, heralded by the General Strike of 1926. Men were laid off, and as the *Clifton Chronicle* reported on the day the strike ended: "Thank God, thank God escaped the lips of one working man from Hotwells who had been unwillingly deprived of his right to work by the closing down of his factory."

By the late Twenties, Hotwells had run down again, and the dismal slum housing, especially on the Clifton Wood side of the Hotwell Road, with its narrow run-down courts and alleys, was crying out for clearance.

Eventually Love Street, the section from Trinity Church to Dowry Square, was demolished in the Thirties to build Hillsborough Flats, pronounced the very latest thing in council housing.

The Depression affected Clifton proper only marginally, in that some families financially dependent on trade and commerce had to reduce their life style. But it hit Hotwells with bitter force. Pensioners still alive remember the way the women and children had to char and sew and run errands and chop sticks to keep the family alive while the man was out of work, and they recall the bitterness of being dependent on Clifton charity. The poverty was marked, and the Church Army set up a hostel in Dowry Square, and held concerts in the gardens on Saturday nights, to cheer people up.

Local traders would give credit they could hardly afford, and one woman remembered her mother fainting in a Hotwells shop, because she had not eaten for days. The hated means test reduced life to mere existence. Soap box orators said as much on the triangle of land known as Soapy Park, at the bottom of Granby Hill.

Though Bristol as a whole was hit less hard than other industrial cities, it was estimated in 1938 that 40,000 people were living in poverty and a proportion of these certainly lived in Hotwells. A standard of living survey by Bristol University compared Clifton College boys' health and physical development with working class children and found them taller and heavier. There were cases of TB and malnutrition among Hotwells children in the late Thirties.

For distraction from the misery, there was still the cinema, which began to take over from live entertainment. The ABC Whiteladies was built in 1923 behind an existing frontage and was thought very luxurious. "Here one need not dream of

E.H. YOUNG'S CLIFTON

A steep street where narrow fronted old houses informed the public that apartments were to be let within, brought her to the broad space of trees and grass called The Green. Straight ahead of her was the wide street flanked by houses of which her home was one – a low white building hemmed in on each side by another, and with a small walled garden in front of it; not a large house, but one full of character and of quiet self-assurance. These houses, all re-christened in a day of enthusiasm, Nelson Lodge, with Trafalgar House, taller, bigger but not so white, on one side of it, and Hardy Cottage, somewhat smaller, on the other, had faced open meadows in General Mallett's boyhood.

The Misses Mallett, 1922.

It was the last day of April and the trees were green. There was no lack of them in this which had once been the fasionable part of Radstowe and now was half business district and half slum. On the steep ascent from the river to the heights of Upper Radstowe they were everywhere: there was an avenue of them in a wide square where dirty children played on the pavements and slatternly women stood in the doorways of panelled halls: they towered above tiny houses, they looked over high brick walls of gardens, now overgrown and decorated with drying garments of the poor, and William Nesbitt, toiling up a narrow tortuous lane, renewed his sensation of climbing through a wood where half the trees were houses and half the houses trees.

E.H. Young, *William*, 1925.

SHOPPING IN CLIFTON, 1930s

Mrs Doubleday bought a pound of apples, reminded Mrs Stone that evergreens and flowers would be welcome for the church decorations and continued down The Barton, a street which was characteristic of Upper Radstowe. The shops, which were chiefly on one side, had been built against the lower part of tall old houses, and, from a distance, the severe pediments of these could be seen above the smaller,

later growth. And the shops too were characteristic. Except for the flower shop and a fishmonger's, they were small and unpretentious, their owners were not agitated by requests for commodities they did not keep, or zealous in procuring them. They continued to be amiably regretful, and the shops continued to survive, as though this were a village without a rival within many miles.

E.H. Young, *The Curate's Wife*, 1934.
[The Barton is the Mall]

GOOD WORKS, 1930s

The party settled down at a long table in a room upstairs. Mrs Doubleday went to the cupboards in the walls as if she owned them and drew out bundles of calico and flannel, and Dahlia sat with her thimble in front of her until she was supplied with some puzzling parts of a shirt. 'Tack up the seams' said Mrs Doubleday, 'and take them to Miss Fairweather to be stitched.' Miss Fairweather with an ostracised expression sat behind a sewing machine at a small table apart.
Suddenly an authoritative voice boomed over a large bosom at the end of the table. "We must have sideshows. Fortune tellers, little plays, competitions ... what we want to avoid is making this a parochial affair. We want to attract the whole of Upper Radstowe. Even some of the other suburbs,' she conceded, "People from across the Downs, people from Coombe Friars [Abbots Leigh]. We must concentrate more on the side shows. That's where we shall make money. If we're not careful, this will be nothing but a Sale of Work. A Sale of Work!

E.H. Young, *The Curate's Wife*, 1934.

DECAY IN CLIFTON

The houses in Upper Radstowe had a way of growing shabby and when Hannah stood at the gate peering in, she fancied that thus the ghosts of the 18th century must stand and look at their fine houses going to decay, let out in flats, with the gathered perambulators and the bicycles of the inhabitants cumbering the stately entrance halls.

E.H. Young, *Miss Mole*, 1930.

THE GENERAL STRIKE, May 3–12, 1926

One way Cliftonians can assist in lightening the transport difficulties is by taking home their purchases from Clifton shops and not insisting on delivery. A wise economy in the use of lighting and fuel should also be observed. No-one should adopt the selfish practice of hoarding food. Everybody who feels he or she could assist in the maintenance of the essential services should give in their names at the Central Library. The phrase Business As Usual has again come into force and it is our duty to impress on Cliftonians the need for carrying out the exclusive advice of Lord Stanhope: Keep Cheerful.

***Clifton Chronicle*. [The strike delayed a visit from the Prince of Wales who was due to open the Portway]**

THE CHAPEL WAY OF LIFE

Hope Chapel was my father's life, he was a deacon and a teacher and we attended three times on Sundays and most nights of the week – socials, meetings, choir practice, three day sales every year. I was married there and my children were christened there. One rule that Lady Hope laid down was that the Chapel could never be demolished.

Mollie Sweeney.

USING WHITELADIES ROAD PUBLIC LIBRARY, circa 1920

There was no open access to books; you looked up a catalogue, made a note of the number and went to a glass case containing many hundreds of numbers with a slot against each. If the slot was empty the book was available and you went to the desk and asked for it. The library ticket was about one inch wide and three inches long. The attendant took this away and slipped it into the slot correct for its number, so that everyone would know the book was out. When you returned it, the whole process was reversed.

Anne Edbrooke-Ballard.

dwelling in marble halls," said the *Western Daily Press*, "but can enjoy the reality." The Embassy in Queen's Avenue opened in 1933, and with 2,100 seats was the largest in the West.

Hotwells had its cinema still, now a bit of a flea-pit and converted for talkies, and for live entertainment, Hotwells had the Albert Hall – was this a joke? – a tiny building still there on North Green Street. Mainly entertainment came via the chapel and Sunday school, for there were by then six chapels and mission halls in the district.

And then just as the end of the Depression seemed in sight came another war.

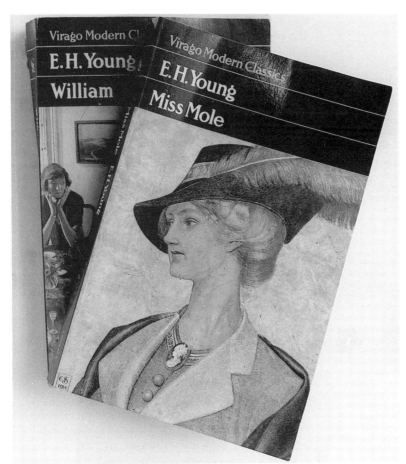

86. The plaque at Number 2, Saville Place.

87. E.H. Young's novels are enjoying a revival, with re-publication by Virago Press.

They heard their mother calling from below. 'Dahlyer-r! Jennifer-r!' she cried and Jenny gave her father's quick little frown. She hoped the neighbours would not hear their names pronounced in an unmistakable Radstowe accent.

E.H. Young, *Jenny Wren,* **1932.**

88. Industrialised Hotwells in
the 1920s.

89. A poetic portrait of
the Zig Zag.

90. The Downs with the Royal Show pavilion in 1913.

91. The Zoo in 1909.

92. Comfortable Canynge Road in 1914.

93. Run-down Hotwells: Dowry Square with the Church Army hostel on the left.

94. Shopping in Queen's Road in the 1930s.

95. Love Street, Hotwells before road widening. The buildings on the right were replaced by the present Hillsborough flats.

96. Panoramic Clifton.

Full circle

Few Cliftonians realised that even before the Second World War broke out, there were top secret plans to run the entire west region from some bomb-proofed cellars at 18 and 19 Woodland Road.

There the regional commissioner, Sir Hugh Elles, laid his plans, documented in a highly secret war book. In it were details on how the west would cope under Nazi occupation. The BBC, supposedly in its bomb-proof tunnel on the Portway, would broadcast instructions on what to do, local schoolchildren would run messages, stockpiles of food were ready in secret dumps, all the wells and springs had been listed, as had the names of printers who could prepare leaflets. He had even written detailed instructions on what to do about prisoners in west jails, and on how to dig mass graves.

The Ministry of Information, a misleading title, set up its offices in Belgrave Road, where throughout the war, propoganda and carefully censored information was fed to the press and the public.

The BBC was evacuated to Bristol and most of these exotic bow-tied sherry-drinking folk came to billets in Clifton; when Clifton College was evacuated to Bude, in February 1941, the BBC took over Watson's House – and apparently left it in a disgraceful condition when they went.

Various church halls were taken over as recording studios and 'Garrison Theatre' was recorded in All Saints Hall in Victoria Square and early episodes of ITMA were made in Portland Street. Famous faces suddenly appeared in the shops and small autograph hunters were in paradise. Conductor Adrian Boult and the BBC Symphony Orchestra arrived and tested the acoustics in the Portway tunnel, which was to become a major bone of contention later on.

Bristol Corporation had plans for the Portway tunnel, which was part of the defunct Port and Pier railway. They bomb-proofed part of it for storing the city treasures and archives and the rest was to be given over to the BBC for an emergency station in the event of German occupation.

But local people had different plans. When the air raids started in May 1940, a committee headed by St. John Reade, a master at Clifton College, went to the Corporation to ask that the tunnel be opened and prepared as a shelter. When this was refused, in November they simply moved in, and the tunnel became famous as the safest place in the west country. People flocked to it from far and wide and as many as 3,000 would turn up in the evening hoping for a place in a tunnel which should have held no more than 200 or so.

Fights broke out, the Corporation tried to get the police to move the people out, and the whole matter went to Cabinet level, as Sir Hugh Elles tried as he put it to "winkle" the shelterers out. An attempt to move the BBC equipment in failed because of a sit-in.

One user remembers: "You couldn't lay out, you stood up or knelt, cooped up with your back against the wall, and it was always streaming with water. We couldn't sleep, sleep was almost impossible, any sleeping was done during the day, at school or at home. Because there were no doors in the tunnel you couldn't close it off and people would arrive in the night, especially when a raid was taking place. It was sheer panic."

But at least war provided some social glue – the working class users of the shelters noticed with surprise that the snootiest Cliftonians who came to the damp and smelly Portway tunnel or who sat on the cold steps of the Clifton Rocks Railway shelters became human during the air raids, and joined in the entertainments and singing.

For Clifton, like the rest of Bristol, was severely hammered by the raids of 1940 and 1941. The major loss was Park Street, where 13 buildings on the east side and eight on the west side were totally destroyed and almost every other one burned out or seriously damaged – though there were some who escaped unscathed: George's Bookshop at the top, lost just one book, cut by glass.

Berkeley Square lost one side, in the Triangle the cinema and Lennards were flattened; the Museum, the University and the Coliseum were all badly damaged.

The village itself came off fairly lightly, apart from the loss of the parish church; though incendiaries damaged seven houses in Cornwallis Crescent, and 18 in Royal York Crescent (one house had to be completely rebuilt inside) and took out one house in Richmond Terrace, the only major high explosive bomb to fall in Clifton village was on the corner of Merchants Road. The modern infilling as a result of

that hit is all too evident today.

There was some damage in Whiteladies Road, mainly to churches, and All Saints Church lost its spire for good; in Hotwells, Trinity Church received a direct hit and there was damage in Dowry Parade, Chapel Row and Joy Hill. Repairs were done and the gaps were slowly filled in during the austerity Forties and Fifties, but progress was very slow.

The war started what you might call the Bohemianisation of Clifton. As well as the BBC's pipe-smoking artistic types and the actors and comedians, there were the Americans.

When the Yanks arrived to make their west headquarters in Clifton College, and lay the plans for D-Day, another element was added to the social mix. The University students and staff took on wartime work that broadened their social experience, and all this was to have its effect after the war.

The Americans made a conscious effort to mingle with the locals and entertain their children, and they were a great attraction to the local girls, who went with them to the Red Cross club set up at the Royal West of England Academy, and to tea dances at the Berkeley. Hotwells had a forces club too, at St. George's Hall, and in the summer, dancing the jitterbug on College Green was a highlight of the week.

When the end of the war came, Clifton was a shadow of its former grand self. The gradual downgrading of the Georgian terraces, the decay and neglect made worse by bomb damage, had turned Clifton shabby, and the whole nature of the population changed.

The elderly and the less well-off remained, but the more prosperous middle class started moving out, landlords started buying up the houses to turn into cheap flats and bedsitters. The proximity to the University meant that in the Fifties Clifton became a student quarter, full of drab and slummy flats and bedsitters. It was horrifying to the old guard, but Clifton became trendy among the young and the artistic, who liked its seedy charm.

In the Fifties and early Sixties the village was still very much a real shopping centre, with five butchers, four bakers, five small grocers, three hardware shops, a Co-op, a Liptons and a Home and Colonial, a tailor, Mr Neshitch, an old-fashioned draper, Mr Prosser, and had only one antique shop and one restaurant, the Swiss Gourmet.

Not surprisingly, student Clifton led the way: it had the first espresso bar, the Nightingale, in a

JULIE BOWEN REMEMBERS WARTIME IN CLIFTON

We lived in the Triangle, Clifton, through all the raids; the house wasn't hit but masonry fell on the roof and the windows were broken so we lived downstairs. There was a surface shelter in Berkeley Square which we used when the raids were really bad, we had to run across the road to get to it, but most of the time we sheltered under the stairs. I was terribly nervous, I used to scream while the raids were on, I was paranoid about them. I was a mass of nerves, I thought German paratroopers would land on our flat roof and get in through the windows and kill us.

I went to Christchurch school which was what is now the Clifton Library. The school had no shelter of its own, so whenever the siren went we had to run in a crocodile to Portland Street Drill Hall, about 150 of us. My education certainly suffered because of the raids. I couldn't concentrate, and I didn't sleep properly, so I didn't learn as much as I should have done. It was a very strict school, you were seen and not heard and no excuses were accepted. The teaching was good, the teachers were dedicated, but they were old-fashioned in their teaching methods. Sunday school was very important to me; it was held in Berkeley Place after St. Andrews was bombed, in what is now the dance studios. There we had stories and readings and made plasticine models and played with felt pictures.

Food in the war was so boring – we knew what luxury was because my uncle worked at Cater Stoffel and Forts in Queen's Road [it closed in the Sixties] and to us it was like Harrods with its marble floors and oak surrounds. When Lease Lend started, he brought us our first jar of Heinz sandwich spread and it was wonderful – such luxury. We spent long hours queuing for basic necessities like bread, which was grey and dirty and looked and tasted like asbestos. I minded not having a birthday cake or bananas and I remember our wonder when the Americans who were billeted at Clifton College provided a party for the children of Christchurch School. There was actually ice cream and jelly and cake and chocolate and Walt Disney cartoons. We had never seen anything like it, it was FABULOUS.

MASS OBSERVATION REPORT ON THE PORTWAY TUNNEL SHELTER, DECEMBER 1940

There is no sign but two printed paper notices with an arrow pointing in. Just inside there is a blast wall of sandbags. As one enters, the stench is overpowering, a mixture of sandbags, urine, disinfectant, sweat and bedding. For about the first 50 yards one has to walk through water two inches deep, over bumps in the ground. On each side, beds are standing in water. Sometimes blankets or an old mac is placed on the mud. This water is spring water and comes from a spring where people fill their kettles. It is a simple business to divert this water out but Bristol Corporation has refused them permission. Consequently all night long water is pouring into the shelter like a miniature waterfall. Farther along it is drier, and there is great congestion. About half a dozen families have tent arrangements of sackcloth thereby ensuring a certain stuffy privacy. A little over half way along there is another brick wall. Beyond this the walls are whitewashed and bunks four across have been built. The poorest and dirtiest people of them are using this end. The children are four to a bunk. Lighting is by candles and oil lamps. Some distance from the other end is a brick wall with sackcloth; on the other side are the closets labelled M and W. The closets are never empty for more than 30 seconds at a time; they have to serve 1,000 people. There is a stinking tang of chlorine. Beyond is the open air."

CLIFTON PARISH CHURCH BOMBED, NOVEMBER, 1940

Two hundred to three hundred people sheltered in the crypt there. During the November 24/25 raid they sang hymns to a piano and violin accompaniment until the building above became too hot for safety. The next day a notice went up on the ruins "Cast down but not destroyed."
"I remember walking up Constitution Hill a day later after the bombing of Clifton Parish Church on my way to school at La Retraite and crying as I saw the smouldering remains of the church."

basement in Berkeley Place, the first continental delicatessen, run by the Polish Mr Lodowski in Princess Victoria Street, the first antiques market and the first Chinese restaurant, in the Triangle. In the Greyhound, a pub for the louche and sophisticated, at various times in the Sixties you would find sculptor David Backhouse, actor Peter O'Toole (he had lodgings on Granby Hill) playwright-to-be Tom Stoppard and novelist-to-be Angela Carter.

And as the Sixties progressed and affluence grew, gentrification reached the Clifton agenda. The students who had pigged it there grew up and married and started buying the big terrace houses for what now seem derisory sums, did them up and let rooms to other students. Bit by bit the improvements went on through the Seventies, until Royal York Crescent, which had become horribly shabby, was a smart address once more. Now all the crescents and terraces are genteel again, fully restored, and students can't afford to live in Clifton any longer.

The Clifton and Hotwells Improvement Society was revived in 1968. The earlier 1900s one had concerned itself with publicising Clifton as a resort, planting trees and buying benches and putting on concerts but the new CHIS was concerned with planning and conservation. It was needed, too, for the council in the late Fifties and through the Sixties were anti-conservation and some of the seedier bits of Clifton and Hotwells were threatened with demolition. The rot virtually stopped in 1972, when Clifton and part of Hotwells was declared a conservation area, the second in the city.

But before then, late eighteenth century houses on Granby Hill that would now be treasured and completely restored were knocked down, and insensitive infilling was allowed in gaps left by bombs. Victorian buildings came down to make way for modern office blocks, and it was not until the late Sixties and early Seventies that public pressure and a few more conservation-minded planners saved Clifton from any more destruction.

By far the most outrageous episode was the city planners' outline permission in 1971 for the Avon Gorge Hotel to build a £1½ million garage and hotel room block in the Gorge, close to the Suspension Bridge. The plan was passed with suspicious haste because a government grant of £126,000 was at stake if work was started by May that year.

When the planning decision became public, there was an uproar of protest. Despite a postal strike,

DANGERS OF CLIFTON

Sir, Your reader protests against the proposal to demolish the war bombed Clifton Church on the ground that children can climb up to the top of the tower and risk falling. He dismissed this reason as 'nonsense almost amounting to hypocrisy' and describes the children as 'probably fictitious.' I notice that the protestor lives in Sea Mills Park. I live next door to the church.

Arthur Bristol, Bishop of Bristol, Bishop's House, Clifton. EP, Oct 1952.

CANYNGE SQUARE

It had seen better days. It was evident in the delicate tracery of the fanlights over the doors and the wrought iron balconies breaking the plain fronts here and there, but now most of the houses were in need of paint, and, though there were no printed cards in the windows, advertising lodgings to be let, the shabby young clerks who blossomed out into bright sports clothes at weekends and the old ladies with the over-trimmed hats who took their slow daily walks were certainly not householders. Fashion and prosperity had deserted this corner of Upper Radstowe where all the houses had basement kitchens and anyone walking round the Square at cooking times would have seen these caverns lighted as though for some underground festivity.

E.H. Young, *Chatterton Square*, 1947.

ANGELA CARTER ON CLIFTON IN THE SIXTIES

"The auction sales were held in the gutted corpse of what had once been an Edwardian department store, where tall, thin pillars topped with fading garlands of gilded leaves insinuated hints of departed elegancies among the heaped junk around them and strangely placed long mirrors, flyblown, in dark corners, suddenly astonished you with your own speckled reflection.

Morris sucked up eagerly the smell of dirt, poverty and graveclothes; blindfolded he could have recognised the smell of an auction sale. He loved the smell. He loved junk . . . the best times of his life were the dark nights when in Honeybuzzard's van, they went secretly to the deserted condemned old houses which the city council planned shortly to demolish, and by the light of guttering candles, would sort over and pick about in all their dead flotsam."

***Shadow Dance*. 1966.**

MODERN TIMES

Battling Jean Tidy, chairman of the Mall Residents' Association said: "You can get drunk from one end of Clifton to the other but you can't buy a needle and thread."

She has a casualty list of the traditional traders who have closed up shop on Clifton in the past decade or so. These include two butchers, the Co-op supermarket, the Woolworths store, a newsagent, two delicatessens, two greengrocers, a fish shop and two ironmongers. In their place have come antique dealers, silversmiths, jewellers, estate agents, banks, building societies, off-licences, pubs and restaurants. "There are 27 drinking places in Clifton village – 44 if you count the restaurants – and seven off-licences. We are very tolerant people but enough is enough. When the pubs turn out at night, it's like Soho, and the traffic has become unspeakable."

Iain Patterson, the city's Planning officer said: "Clifton is the victim of its own success in many ways. Houses which were near slums have been converted into six or even eight high quality flats which attract car-owning residents. But the frontage of a Georgian house is only 24 feet."

Bristol Evening Post, Feb 1982.

97. Some things never change: walking on the Downs.

thousands of letters were delivered by hand to Environment Minister Peter Walker.

In the end the plan was called in and a nine day public inquiry was held. Among those to give evidence was poet and Clifton-lover John Betjeman. 'Lords, Artists And Actors Join In Protest' said the *Evening Post* headline and petitions from 782 students, 57 actors and 173 artists were handed in. Botanist Dr. Lewis Frost claimed the hotel would be a threat to the Common Polypody, not to mention Chinsia and Autumn Squill, Round-headed Leek and Spiked Speedwell.

Betjeman, who had lived for a few months in Clifton as a young man, was a star turn at the hearing, according to the *Western Daily Press*: "The giant hotel planned for the Avon Gorge is old-fashioned and a monster, poet and author Sir John Betjeman said yesterday. Sir John broke into a Cornish holiday to make the special journey to Bristol. He was the star attraction of Day Four and took on the role of personal guardian of Bristol's heritage."

"The great thing about Bristol, which makes it unique – and to me the most interesting city in England – is that it has got this natural scenery in the middle of it, crossed by that marvellous suspension bridge," he said.

It was an asset that made him obliged to come to give evidence. "I object to the idea of a hotel on the Avon Gorge and regard it as completely unsuitable. . . . It is more important to preserve the views and assets of a famous old city than benefit a few people who will be able to afford to stay in such a monster.

"I can't believe that the millions of people who come and will continue to come to places like this will really allow one commercial company to make such enormous profits of private development when the whole city will have to suffer."

In the end the plan was thrown out with great jubilation but the hotel's ambitions did not end there; they tried again with a plan for a modern low rise wing and that too was turned down.

The planning vandalism went on: a scheme to close the docks and fill them in, or bridge them at Mardyke and run a tunnel under Brandon Hill to Whiteladies Road also bit the dust, on grounds of cost as well as philistinism.

Still run-down Hotwells suffered another blow in the early Sixties when 80 families were moved out of their mainly Georgian homes, which were demolished to make way for the necessary but ugly Cumberland Basin flyover scheme.

There are still planning tussles in Clifton, over traffic policy and parking, change of use to offices, and over the excessive number of eating and drinking establishments. When the old Regent Street Post office which had been in the 1850s building since the turn of the century was closed in 1988 on the somewhat specious grounds that the floor was unsafe (the block was due for redevelopment and needed emptying) there was a petition with 2,000 signatures.

Another public protest saved the old Pump Room at the Avon Gorge from redevelopment and there is a brave plan to revive the Rocks Railway for tourists and bring back the paddle steamers. Trying to get back what has been lost or demolished is a constant Clifton and Hotwells preoccupation.

So the wheel has come full circle and once more Clifton thinks of itself as a tourist attraction just as it did in the eighteenth century. The old service shops have disappeared to be replaced by boutiques, restaurants, wine bars, antique shops, gift shops – you can't buy basic things like a needle and cotton any more. In the 1980s property boom, one Clifton house in Sion Hill went on the market for half a million pounds.

Hotwells and Clifton Wood, too, have had their mini-gentrification and the big Georgian houses that were apartments for the visitors to the spa are now back to an equivalent elegance and glory. The Nineties image of the area is very much what it always was in the past, of a wealthy, exclusive, expensive suburb, where arty, well-off people live in big gracious houses.

And the old charge of snobbery remains, witness this letter to the *Evening Post*, published in March, 1992.

"So the good burghers of Clifton village have decided to have gold lettered waste bins. I suppose their binmen will be dressed by Hardy Amies and the refuse lorries will be specially scented by Chanel. Come off it, my good men of Clifton and Hotwells Improvement Society, you've got more money than sense. Your rubbish is the same as everyone else's."

98. & 99. Lennard's
Corner in the Triangle: lost
in the blitz.

100. St. Andrew's Church, Clifton, blitzed and finally demolished in the 1950s. Seen from the lime walk.

101. The shock of the new: the striking modernity of Clifton Cathedral, consecrated in 1973.

102. 1964: not blitz damage, but neglect. This side of Hope Square had to be rebuilt, and conservationists saved the rest.

103. & 104. A triumph for people over bureaucracy. An artist's impression of how the planned development would look, and the public call to action.

126

106. A splendid survivor: the chemist on the corner of West Mall.

105. One of the few traditional suppliers to open shop in recent years.

107. Closed in 1988 after serving Clifton for over 80 years.

108. The new Clifton: wine bars and boutiques.

Also available

TO BUILD THE SECOND CITY
Architects and craftsmen of Georgian Bristol

Timothy Mowl

Asked which city, Bath or Bristol, had the wider range and variety of fine classical buildings, most people – Bristolians included – would choose Bath. And, as Timothy Mowl emphatically shows, they would be wrong. Bristol in general, Clifton in glorious particular, are the unexplored, undervalued treasure houses of 18th century design. The reason for the neglect is the paradoxical one that most of their 'Georgian' architecture was built in the 19th century.

Bristol's architectural development would be more easily explained if the city were built on some large island out in the Bristol Channel near Lundy. Nothing here is predictable in national terms.

In the first decade of the 18th century, a cheerfully corrupt City Corporation plunged a stone and timber Bristol back into a Dark Age of brick. When most of England was going Palladian, Bristol handed itself over to a Scottish architect with an intensely individual and subtle feeling for the Baroque. Then William Halfpenny, celebrated elsewhere only for his jejeune pattern books, was allowed in Bristol to design substantial buildings of extraordinary charm, both Gothick and widely indeterminate.

Gripped by a clan of craftsmen-builders in the middle years of the century the city nevertheless produced, with all the unexpectedness of a conjurer's rabbit, a small Rococo palazzo whose imaginative sophistication can be paralleled only in continental Europe.

Finally, after Waterloo, Bristol architects realised that the romantic grandeur of its tidal gorge presented the ideal site for a new classical city of casual excellence. The result was Clifton, a suburb that most who know all three rate above both Robert Adam's Edinburgh and John Wood's Bath.

Available from bookshops at £19.95 hardback.